GRIEF AND LOSS

Healing techniques to go through loss of a loved one

Grief and loss copyright © 2016

All rights reserved. No part of this publication may be reproduced, distributed, or transmitted in any form or by any means, including photocopying, recording, or other electronic or mechanical methods, without the prior written permission of the publisher, except in the case of brief quotations embodied in critical reviews and certain other noncommercial uses permitted by copyright law.

Table of Contents

INTRODUCTION V
Chapter 01: UNDERSTANDING GRIEF 1
Chapter 02: THE FIVE STAGES OF GRIEF AND LOSS 17
Chapter 03: EMBRACING YOUR FEELINGS 27
Chapter 04: MANAGEMENT OF GRIEF/DISTRESS 39
Chapter 05: REBUILDING YOUR ROUTINE 49
Chapter 06: TURNING LOSS INTO HEALING 59
Chapter 07: FINDING PEACE 65
Chapter 08: DETOURS ARE FRUSTRATING 75
Chapter 09: SAYING GOOD-BYE TO THE OLD ROAD 79
Chapter 10: SETTING MY SIGHTS ON A NEW DIRECTION 87
Chapter 11: HEADING FOR A CLEAR ROAD AHEAD 93
Chapter 12: MOVING ON 101
CONCLUSION 105

INTRODUCTION

Are undergoing a loss of a loved one—a spouse, a partner, a parent, a child, or someone else who had been a vital part of your life and about whom you cared deeply? Has your loss left you sad, confused, angry, and full of questions that seem to have no answers?

If any of these examples describe your current situation, chances are that you are experiencing grief, a natural, normal response to encountering any major loss. Grief is an emotional distress that you suffer when someone or something close to you has been taken away. It is a multidimensional experience that can affect you physically, emotionally, socially, and even spiritually. Grief can come upon women or men at any age or stage of life, and it cuts across all socioeconomic levels. No one escapes loss; whatever your philosophical or spiritual belief system, experiencing a significant loss and the subsequent grieving can shake up your psyche.

When grief strikes, it can feel as if the world has been pulled out from under you. The sudden onset of deep sorrow can occur whether you had time to prepare for a loss or whether it roared in without warning. You might wonder if the dark storm clouds will ever disappear. You may even find yourself replaying the same thoughts over and over in your mind:

Researchers suggest that adjusting to the death of a loved one is probably the biggest adjustment we'll need to make in our lives. This book focuses on grief following the death of a person you loved, how grief changes your life's journey, what the grief experience is like, and how you can use this forced detour called grieving to develop a revised life course that can become rich and rewarding again.

Grief causes a major detour on your life's journey because it is a natural response on your part to loss. Life ends; grieving the death of your loved one begins. Perhaps you are saying to yourself, "I have been grieving already!" because your loved one experienced an extended illness that led to death.

Loved ones surrounding the dying person do grieve losses of function as the person is no longer able to do what he or she was previously able to do. We would contend that grieving those functional losses does not replace the need to grieve the person's actual death. No one can grieve the physical absence of the person until he or she actually dies.

Grief doesn't wait for you to invite it into your life when someone you love has died. It happens automatically and universally. Now, with the death of your loved one, you are forced to travel a detour rather than your intended route. You generally don't choose a route that you know will have a detour. You probably try to avoid detours, at almost any cost.

In this book we use the analogy of your life as being on a road trip, and now, with the death of your loved one, you are forced to travel the detour of grieving.

This book is focused totally on recovery from the emotional pain caused by death. For all of you struggling with unresolved grief issues of a loved one, I know that the actions outlined in this book will lead you to completion of the pain caused by this loss. I also know that recovery is not an easy journey. I know that your losses may have closed your heart down. If I could, I would be with you as you take the actions that will lead your heart to open again. You may be afraid to start, or you may get scared along the way. Please remember that hundreds of thousands of people have used these same actions. I know that they join us in encouraging you to move through your apprehension and begin the process of recovery.

CHAPTER 01
UNDERSTANDING GRIEF

What is grief?

It is a normal but deeply painful response to loss

Why Does Grief Happen?

Why does grief occur when someone dies? There are three primary reasons why this grief experience is happening to you:

1. Because you loved that person. Loving someone means that you were attached to him or her and cared deeply about that person. Hopefully the relationship and feelings were reciprocal. You knew each other well—what lay at each other's hearts.

2. Because you formed a relationship with that person. You likely experienced an emotional interweaving with the other person—he or she was someone you could count on and with whom you had connected. You probably gave to and received many things from that relationship. Perhaps there were physical aspects you will miss—the hugs and touches, or if you were married, the sexual intimacy. Even if your relationship wasn't the healthiest or most satisfying, that doesn't mean you won't grieve. You still experience a loss.

3. Because some part of your lifestyle was affected by your loved one's presence. You grieve not only the person's death but also the end of the life you had lived with that person. That includes all you did together and all that came as a result of having that person in your life. No matter what role the person played in your life, you are now forced to recognize that your life will change dramatically in those areas that involved that person.

How Do I Get Rid of the Pain and Get Back to Normal?

Grief needs an active, intentional decision to face the pain of the loss. We are amazed at the number of people who seem to let grief overtake them and then passively wait, thinking grief will eventually end without doing anything to help end it. We think this is because they don't know what to do. Using our own personal experiences and our professional knowledge of the grief process, we would like to help you work through grief.

Take, for example, a person who falls and breaks a leg. The broken leg will hurt. The person does not decide to experience pain—it comes naturally. The pain of grief comes just as naturally when a loved one dies. But just as the physical pain of a fracture usually motivates a person to do something about the injury (like going to the doctor, taking pain medication, getting a cast applied, or having surgery), hope-fully the pain of grief will motivate you to do something to help you along the grief process.

The basic premise of this book is that a grieving person needs to intentionally engage in healthy and helpful actions to address their grief in order to move through grieving and discover a fulfilling life once again. The passing of time is a necessary element in the grief process, but it's not enough by itself.

Healthy grieving takes deliberate, intentional actions coupled with time in order for a person to effectively heal after a death.

With a loved one's death, grief often rolls over you like an overpowering wave sucking you down to the bottom and making you feel like there is nothing left—familiar landmarks are gone with no reason to go on. It's a very overwhelming and painful experience to have to deal with, so we want you to understand a little more clearly what your grief will probably look and feel like. This grief journey is often described as a slow process ultimately moving in a positive direction but coupled with intermittent "lows" or "valleys" that may seem like a step backward. Remember, grieving is not a consistently upward linear process. Grief is more like waves on the ocean—the waves ebb and flow as storms, winds, and tides change. Grieving takes at least a year, and most likely a few more, to complete. That is because discovering out that you are without your loved one takes time and hard work.

Your grief journey is unique, and there is no uniform way to grieve because of all the individual factors in your life in contrast to others, such as your own and your deceased loved one's personalities, the type of relationship you had together, the type of death your loved one experienced, your present individual life circumstances, and how soon you began doing intentional grief work. But regardless of all your individual life circumstances, there are five universal components to grief that you may well encounter on your grief de-tour. Research has clearly demonstrated that the experience of grief triggers aspects of all of the following five responses for almost everyone.

1. Physical. Changes occur in eating and exercise patterns, frequently with a lack of desire to do either. Sleep becomes problematic and is often interrupted by thoughts of the de- ceased. A bereaved person is usually at a higher risk for illness and even death because the stress of loss and the physical and emotional drain of grieving lowers one's immune system, making good self-care so important.

2. Emotional. A grieving person often experiences a flood of emotions including, of course, sadness, but also anger, fear, anxiety, guilt, regret, relief, loneliness, and a myriad of other feelings, many of which seem overwhelming and worrisome.

3. Cognitive. The way a person thinks is usually affected by grief. Some people may make impulsive decisions or not be able to make any decisions at all. The advice to wait at least one year before making major decisions is well founded.

Memory is disrupted, especially short-term; a person may not remember from one moment to the next what he or she was getting ready to do or who called on the phone. The ability to focus and concentrate is often disrupted. All of this often pools into a terror that the mourning person is "going crazy."

4. Behavioral. Typical patterns of behavior are often disrupted. A person may go from one extreme to the other in their behaviors. For example, he or she may either refuse to leave their house or fight against going home. The individual may have a difficult time returning to work or may throw himself or herself completely into work in an effort to distract from the grief experience. The bereaved person may lack motivation to accomplish even routine household responsibilities like opening the mail or doing the laundry. Apathy, withdrawal, and procrastination are also common occurrences.

5. Spiritual. Invariably, questions about one's spiritual faith and continuing purposes in life are raised by the death of a loved one. Even if a person is not particularly religious, death may force him or her to examine their belief about life after

Tasks of grieving are something like that. These tasks are five interrelated goals that need to be accomplished or experienced for a person to move through the grief process into a full, healthy, and rewarding life following the death of a loved one (whether that is a spouse, parent, sibling, child, or friend).

They are not sequential in the sense that one task needs to be completed before you begin another. In fact, they are complexly interrelated like a fine symphony, with parts of one task being worked on simultaneously with others. They are not the type of tasks that can be completed quickly or all at once—these tasks are integral to your entire grieving process.

This grief process is like putting a complex puzzle together. There are as many ways of accomplishing this as there are individuals doing it. However, there are designated puzzle pieces to be used in specific relationship to others.

Only when the puzzle is complete can a person sit back and appreciate the entire picture for what it is and declare it to be finished. That is also true of the grief process—it is an individual journey, yet there are the five specific tasks with corresponding behaviors that you need to address to help you move through your grief detour.

So what are these tasks that are necessary to heal from grief?

- First, you need to accept the reality that your loved one has died and is unable to return. This may seem obvious, but emotionally accepting the reality of the death can be a tremendous challenge.
- Second, you need to express all your emotions associated with the death. Keeping the emotions "bottled up" inside

The Grieving Process

The process immediately begins upon the sudden loss of a loved one. A person suffering from grief needs support from friends and family. The grief process can last differently for different people; it depends on the nature of the loss, the person's personality, and the amount and quality of support that the person is getting. The process may involve all or some of the following emotions:

1) Shock

The initial reaction to hearing news about losing someone is shock. This is a normal reaction. It is when the grieving person would feel an extreme numbness and disbelieve. It is during this stage that the people usually fail to make even the simplest of decisions; their minds are totally clouded, and they feel lost.

2) Suffering

There will be a feeling of suffering and it may take a long time before the grieving person would start to feel like his heart is starting to heal. There are a lot of other emotions that encompass suffering, like intense pain and hurt. There will also be a feeling of chaos and being disorganized. Daily routines are interrupted and those who are grieving tend to become anti-social, thinking that the people around them do not understand how they feel.

3) Anger

There is also a feeling of intense anger for being powerless to change the situation or to prevent the loss from happening. Sometimes it is also anger of being abandoned and left behind. In most tragic deaths involving fatal accidents and serious illnesses, there is anger towards the people who caused the accident and towards the doctors who failed to save the lives of their loved ones.

4) Guilt

Guilt is also felt for not having prevented the death or for not doing enough. There will be a lot of crying for people who grieve. Suffering can be the most difficult stage of grief because of the varying levels of emotions sufferers are subjected to. Their emotional stability is disrupted and there are those who will need professional help. It is during this stage that those who are grieving are in denial of their loss. Most of them have this feeling that if they sleep it off, thinking that everything will go away, and that it was all a bad dream. When they wake up and realize that it was not, they suffer some more; so acceptance is quite hard to come by.

5) Recovery

Acceptance will help guide the grieving person en-route to the recovery stage. During this stage, those who are grieving can start reorganizing their lives and restore some form of normalcy. Though, it will never be the same without the loved ones they've lost, they will have to accept that they have to carry on without them. There will be some bouts of loneliness during the process but it is normal since memories of the deceased will always remain. Obstacles Commonly Encountered During the Healing Stage

There are people who get stuck in the denial stage that they have a hard time moving forward to acceptance and eventual healing.

While most people are quick to give comforting and encouraging words such as, "you will be well" or "you have to stay tough", these are not really useful according to expert psychologists. In fact, these words are rarely effective; as they can often mislead the sufferers so they end up denying their grief instead of handling it.

The best way to help people who are grieving is to encourage them to express what they feel. You cannot expect a grieving person to stay strong; he is at a very vulnerable stage right now and what he needs someone to support and to listen. He doesn't need people telling him to stay strong, because, frankly speaking, he cannot stay strong and he needs to let his feelings out instead of bottling them inside of him.

What Happened?

Have you lost a person whom you really treasured? Of course you will go through the grieving process. I know if you have just lost your loved one, you are in a difficult situation right now, having lost someone dear to you, the pain could be overwhelming but you have to go through it. There will be a stage of denial, which is perfectly normal, but after that initial shock, you have to learn to embrace it in order for you to recover from it.

Trust the Grief

In your moment of despair, despite how painful it is, grief should be your "friend" because it will guide you on your way back to normalcy.

Three Major Points to Consider

• Every individual has their own unique way of expressing their grief. You have your own unique way of experiencing and expressing yours. As long as you do not get stuck in a negative emotion, you just continue to embrace grief.

• You are set to experience a roller-coaster ride of emotions. Grief does not have exact manifestations. It is unpredictable. There will be moments of silence and peace, and then you might experience a moment of almost reaching the breaking point. It is normal to cry; people in grief always need a good cry.

• Nothing is permanent in this world. You might be overwhelmed by grief today, but tomorrow is another day. You will eventually get over your loss. That's just the way it is.

In order to better cope with grief, it is important that you become aware of the different types of grief.

The death of someone you love is never easy. The extent of your grief depends on two major factors, including how deep your relationship with the person was, and the circumstances surrounding your loss.

The Three Types of Grief

1) Anticipatory Grief

This is when a loved one has been suffering from a long illness and then they finally died. The same kind of grief is felt when an elderly person dies. You somehow expected the outcome and you and the other members of the family prepared for its eventuality. However, even though it is expected, it is still painful. No matter how much one prepares for the death of a loved one, it will always be painful. But, having anticipated it, the members of the family wouldn't have a hard time dealing with grief, and the period of grieving is usually shorter.

Sometimes, when you have witnessed a loved one suffer long enough because of an illness; grief comes with a feeling of relief because you know that your loved one won't be feeling the pain of the illness anymore.

2) Sudden Loss

This type of grief is a complicated one because of the varying circumstances that surround the death of the loved one. It brings about an extreme feeling of shock because the suddenness of the death can be overwhelming. When loved ones meet tragic deaths, those who are left behind find it harder to deal with their loss and they grieve a lot longer.

3) Complicated Grief

This is the type of grief when the process doesn't take its normal course. The intensity of the pain and sadness combined take its toll on the person, most of the time reaching their breaking point. Those who are suffering from this type of grief find it hard to function the way they should, it's like they forgot how it felt like to be "normal". People who go through this kind of grief often end up developing depression and/or anxiety disorder.

Some deaths can be too traumatic for a person to experience. Some deaths that can cause complicated grief are those that resulted from violence or accident, murder, homicide, and suicide.

These deaths are hard to accept, especially the ones that were caused by another person. Most loved ones who were left behind find it hard to process the death of someone they love to heartless people, sometimes, people they don't know of.

A fatal accident resulting to death is also very devastating. The death of a child is also hard on parents.

While others come back from the experience, some get stuck. They would need professional help to resolve their grief.

The Physical and Biological Nature of Grief

Let's look at the evidence of how and why all those frustrating and often frightening manifestations of grief are entirely normal. It is helpful to understand that when you suffer a loss and enter a grieving process, whether or not you are aware of doing so and your body goes into a state of stress. The stress of loss is both mental and physical, disrupting your brain and your biological rhythms. Physiological changes result that can affect your nervous system, your immune system, and even your cardiovascular system. Your whole body can just feel out of sorts.

Physical symptoms of grief may manifest in many different ways. Here are ten of the more frequent experiences for those in the aftermath of a major loss:

1. Loss of appetite. In the first several days or even weeks after enduring a loss, you may find it almost impossible to eat. Regular meals are out of the question, and it may take a great effort on your part even to nibble on the small snacks that others urge you to accept. Your body just isn't interested in food.

2. Stomachaches and nausea. When your nerves are shot from the shock and stress of your loss, it is natural to experience a degree of gastrointestinal distress, even if that symptom was not previously a common one for you.

3. Severe headaches. That pounding in your head is a physical sensation, and it is often accentuated by an emotional response. It is as if some force keeps banging home the reality that your life will never be the same again.

4. Extreme fatigue. Undergoing severe stress can feel as if your body is weighed down by a ton of bricks. No wonder you do not want to leave the house or even get out of bed.

5. Accelerated heart rate or shakiness. Uncertainty about what's going to happen to you in the aftermath of your loss can trigger an increase in adrenaline and a sense of panic resulting in temporarily increased heart rate and/or minor tremors.

6. Difficulty sleeping. When your body is in a state of grief-induced shock, it is hard to settle down into a restful, peaceful state. Sleep may come in fits and starts, often punctuated with endless mind chatter about what happened to you and how the change is making you feel about life.

7. Sudden angry outbursts. Frustrated outbursts that have no immediate trigger can be interpreted as your body's way of expressing its stress overload. Yelling "I can't take this anymore!" or "It's not fair!" may be in part your body's attempt to alleviate grief-related stress.

8. Prolonged crying or sobbing that can briefly trigger a sense of choking. Like other physical symptoms, this sensation can be scary when it occurs. You feel a loss of control and may worry that you are about to suffer something even worse. Try to relax and breathe deeply, reminding yourself that this is another manifestation of grief and your body's attempt to compensate. Within a short time, the sensation will likely pass.

9. Temporary confusion or absentmindedness. If you easily forget the day of the week, or where you left your glasses, or what you had agreed to do an hour ago, this is simply another symptom of the stress caused by your loss. Wandering around your house aimlessly is not a sign that you are "going crazy."

10. Inability to concentrate. You may be watching a movie with your family and suddenly realize that you do not know what happened ten minutes ago, even though you thought you were paying attention.

If you are experiencing a few or several of these physical symptoms, it is helpful to understand that they are often signs of your body's attempt to absorb your grief. You may find that these symptoms will come and go over time, or lessen in their intensity. If you accept what is happening as normal, you can fret about them a little less, which in turn can help to reduce your stress.

Other signs of grief may also be showing up in your day-to-day life. You may notice that you still feel shocked at what happened, even if the loss occurred weeks or even months ago. When you are able to fall asleep, you may be awakened by disturbing dreams of your beloved or whatever you have lost, and you may have waking moments of imagining that your loved one is still here. You may be losing weight, which is not at all surprising if you are having trouble eating. If you are grieving over the loss of a loved one, you may find yourself engulfed by fears of your own mortality. Again, all of these experiences fall into the category of natural and normal responses to grief. Do not be overly concerned that there is something wrong with you. With time, healthy choices, and focused attention on your grief journey, most of the symptoms will likely lessen in frequency and intensity, or eventually dissipate.

You may notice that your loss is having a ripple effect on your life. On top of the actual loss you have suffered, you may be experiencing the loss of a sense of security, the loss of a familiar lifestyle, the loss of status, the loss of a sense of belonging somewhere or with some group, or the loss of a dream. This, too, is part of grief. Major loss usually involves much more than what first meets the eye. The grief triggered by loss can affect everything that you do, and it can show up in every area of your life.

Loss can sometimes come in bunches: the death of a loved one followed by the loss of a job. Multiple losses can send you into compound grief, adding to your despair and anxiety. It is normal and natural that even though you have grieved over one loss, a new loss will still hit you hard. As you thoughtfully begin to redefine all those "different" behaviors and feelings as a normal and necessary part of grieving, you may discover that you are able to relax just a bit more about what you are experiencing.

Part of the healing process is understanding and accepting the reality that your physical and mental state has been disrupted or knocked out of whack, and that it is going to take time and care to return to a more harmonious existence.

Ten Myths and Misconceptions about Grief

A necessary step in successfully managing your grief is to set aside what you may have always believed or what you may have been told by others and confront the myths and misconceptions about grief. Here are ten common myths:

1. Grief should last for a few months or a year at most. There is no right or wrong time frame for the healthy process of grieving to unfold. For many people, the grief process lasts much longer than a year. It will take as long as it needs to take . . . for you. Pressuring yourself to hurry up and get past the grief will actually disrupt the natural healing rhythm of grief and prolong your pain. Instead of counting the weeks or months that you have been grieving, focus your attention and awareness on how well you are practicing the healthy and productive steps related to your grief journey.

2. Grief proceeds through clearly defined stages. You will learn about some of the most common phases or responses to grief after loss, but it is important to understand that these are merely possible reference points on your grief journey. It is entirely possible that some or all of the many phases or forms of grief will not resonate with you. That does not mean you have veered off the trail toward health and healing. It simply means that you are finding your own way.

3. Choosing to pursue counseling for grief is a sign of weakness. Some people find the needed support and guidance to manage the grief process without counseling, but for many others, counseling becomes an essential and invaluable tool in dealing with a loss.

Many of those who benefit from grief counseling had been leading emotionally healthy lives without the need for counseling or therapy before suffering a loss.

They found that, rather than a sign of weakness, choosing counseling for this experience was a sign of wisdom and strength. Counseling helped provide shape and direction to their grief journey and opened the door to a new set of helpful resources and strategies.

4. You need to avoid emotional vulnerability to stay strong for your family. Denying or avoiding your natural emotions slows or even sabotages your healing.

Your family cares about you and wants to see you regain your health and strength. Your willingness to enter fully into the feelings and experiences of grief, along with your ability to explain to your family what you are learning about the realities of the grief journey, will help reassure them that you are on the right track.

5. It is improper to laugh or to feel a profound sense of relief while grieving. It is very natural from time to time to find yourself laughing about the loved one you have lost or the life situation that has been taken away from you. Telling funny stories about the shared past with that person or laughing almost uncontrollably at a private joke you held with them are healthy ways to honor their memory and the love you still feel for them. Crying is not the only form of expressing those feelings. It is also normal to feel a sense of relief that the loss has come, especially if it was preceded by a long period of pain and suffering. The relief does not mean that you "wanted" the loss to come, only that the death or other final point of a life situation at least put an end to one phase of suffering.

6. Grief should be easier if the loss was a long time in coming. Many people are caught by surprise because they assume that if they lose a loved one who is elderly or who had been in the dying stages for months or even years, they are "prepared" for the loss and it won't hurt so much when it comes. The reality is that we grieve the loss itself and the connection we have felt with that person or life situation, regardless of age or manner of passing. While losing a loved one through a sudden accident or illness can certainly be more traumatic, exclusively in the instantaneous result, the sting of a loss is still felt no matter what the circumstances.

7. It won't hurt as much if we remember what was wrong with our relationship with that person or life situation. Many of us have had conflict in our relationship with a parent or another family member, and the difficult feelings about that relationship will not necessarily disappear when that person is gone. However, that doesn't mean the loss won't hurt as much as it would if the relationship had been "perfect." The love that you felt toward that person and the connection you had established will almost inevitably pour through during the grief process. Expecting that it will be lessened because of previous conflicts is usually misguided.

8. It is wrong to suddenly have strong feelings about a loss from a long time ago. This is another natural response during the grief process. As you allow yourself to open up to the deep sadness from your current loss, previous grief related to a loss from long ago may be stirred up. If this happens, welcome it. It may be an opportunity to address unresolved grief from the past, or simply a time to honor the love and connection of someone or something else you have lost.

It does not mean that you love or care any less for whatever you have just lost. You will likely find your attention shifting back to that void soon enough.

9. It is better to just ignore or stifle the pain. Trying to repress your pain is like trying to shut off the water faucet when you have a burst water pipe. It simply will not work. More than that, you are trying to dam up the natural healing process of grief. It is far healthier to allow the pain to be pain, and to find ways of supporting your body and mind through the natural process of grieving.

10. Life will eventually look and feel "normal" again. Loss is permanent. That loved one is not returning. The surgery that removed a part of your body is irreversible. The job or career or other life situation that was lost is still gone. If you are looking for a state of normalcy that is equal to everything returning to the way it used to be, you are setting yourself up for ongoing frustration and disappointment. Change after loss is inevitable. The pain of the loss may never completely go away, although you can certainly expect it to lessen its hold on you. You do have the capacity to rebuild your life, and the potential for joy and happiness will grow over time. But the "old normal" may certainly not return as you come to terms with the "new normal."

If you found yourself believing some or many of these common myths and misconceptions about grief, do not feel bad. These ideas are commonly accepted, and friends and family who mean well may also believe that they are true.

You know better now, and even if it takes a while to let go of the myth, recognize that this too is natural. Learning about grief, and putting into practice what you learn, takes time.

If you had already recognized the reality behind most or even all of these myths, that is a good sign. Nevertheless, you will find it helpful to reinforce those truths as you take new steps forward on your grief journey.

CHAPTER 02
THE FIVE STAGES OF GRIEF AND LOSS

In this life we are living in, will all experience the power nature of grief and loss. This is an inevitable element in life that at some point will all go through. There's no right or wrong way to grieve, and the road to recovery is unique to each person.

The process of grieving is a very sacred and personal time, and should be honored in your own individual way.

Healing takes time and it could be weeks, days, or years before we're able to cope with the loss without being devastated by it. Put simply, it will take as long as it takes.

There are no quick fixes. Sometimes we have to hit rock bottom before we can begin a healing process that is deeply personal to us.

Key Stages of the Grief Process

Denial, Rage or Anger, recovery or Acceptance, bargaining and Acceptance are all parts that forms the stages encountered during the grief process. They are important tools to aid us frame and make out what we could be going through and feeling. However they're not preventions on some linear timeline in grief. Each and every person takes a different path during the grieving process as mentioned earlier in the previous chapters. Not every person will experience all of these stages. My hope is that with these stages comes the understanding of grief's terrain, making you better prepared to deal with life and loss.

DENIAL
Denial forms one of the five stages grief's and has been misapprehended over the years. When this stage of denial was brought in On Death and dying, it mainly focused on the individual who was dying. In this book, On Grief and loss, the individual who may goes through denial is grieving the loss of a loved one. According to an individual who is dying, denial may seem like disbelief. They actually deny the existence of the illness that is going to end their lives. On the other hand, for a person who has lost a loved one, the denial is more symbolic than literal.

This doesn't imply that you literally do not discern your loved one has died. It simply implies that for instance, you go home and you cannot believe that your spouse or your loved one is not going to be in existence anymore. You just can't figure out that he will in no way walk through that door again.

The moment we are in denial, we may at first respond by being paralyzed with distress or filled around with numbness. The denial is still not denial of the real death, although someone may be saying, "I cannot believe he is dead." You will be actually saying to yourself that, at the start because it is too much for his or her mind.

This initial stage of grieving aids us to endure the loss. In this first stage of denial, the world turns out to be worthless and overwhelming. At this moment life seems to makes no sense. We are in a position of shock and disbelief. We go numb. We try to speculate how we can move on without them, and if we can move on, why should we? We try to get an approach that can simply get us through each day. Denial and upset mindedness help us to deal with this horrific situation and make our survival possible. Denial aids us to pace our feelings of grief. It is the way nature of allowing in only as much as we can be able to handle. These feelings are imperative; they're the mind's protective mechanisms. Allowing in all the feelings connected with loss at once would be overwhelming psychologically. We cannot accept what has taken place because we truly can't believe it. To completely believe at this part of the stage would be overwhelming.

The denial mostly comes in the form of our questioning our reality: Isn't true? Did it really come about? Are they truly gone?

Consider the thought that you cannot get over an important person in your life. It is more that you learn to live with the loss and not forget the person.

People frequently find themselves talking about their loss over and over again, which is one way that our psyche copes with trauma. It is a means of denying that act of hurting while trying to acknowledge the actual sense of the loss. As denial fades away, it is gradually replaced with the actual loss, the real fact that someone will never come back again to life.

You start to question the how and why. How did this come about? You may ask over and over again, as you evaluate the situation. You are no longer in an external story-telling manner or mode; now you turn inward as you start the search for comprehending. You look at the circumstances surrounding the loss. Did it have to take place? Did it have to go on that way? Could anything have been done to stop it?

The finality of the loss starts to slowly sink in. She isn't coming back. This time he did not succeed. With each question raised, you start to believe they are really vanished. As you acknowledge the reality of the loss and begin to ask yourself queries, without your knowledge you begin the healing process.

You realize your mind is becoming powerful, and the denial is starting to fade away. But as you carry on, all the emotions and feelings you were denying start to surface.

ANGER

This is another stage of grief that presents itself in numerous ways: anger at your loved one that he did not take better care of himself or be furious that you did not look after him well. Anger doesn't have to be reasonable. You may be mad that you did not see this coming to take place and when you did, there is nothing you could do to prevent it. You may also be mad with the doctors for their incapability of saving someone so dear to you. Also, you can be angry that terrible things could happen to a person whom you valued much.

Anger could also be brought about by you being left behind and you thought you should have more time together. You can tell intellectually that your loved one did not wish to die. However emotionally, all you can tell is that he did die. It was not intended to happen, or at least not at the moment.

It is imperative to recall that the anger fades away once you are feeling safe enough to tell that you will probably endure whatever comes. In the beginning, you experience a shocking environment after you encounter loss. In addition, you encounter engulfment of increasing rage and more emotion and feeling of being unhappy, being alone and panic.

Family and friends are usually taken aback by these feelings, and for the reason that they surface just as you were beginning to handle task at a basic level once more.

Also, you may be annoyed with yourself that you could not stop it from taking place. It isn't that you had the control of preventing it or the willpower to do so but you had the drive motivation in you to help. That drive motivation to save a life is not the power to halt a death. A person once shared, "I'm not happy that I have to go on living in a world where I cannot find her, call her, or see her. I cannot find the one I loved or wanted anywhere. She isn't really where her body is at the moment. The heavenly bodies elude me.

The oneness of her spiritual presence escapes me. I'm lost and full of anger."

Resentment is an essential phase of the healing process. Be ready to experience your anger, though it may look as if it is endless. The more you truly feel it, the more it'll begin to surface and the more you will heal. There are several other feelings under the anger and you will get to them in time, however anger is the feeling we are most used to dealing with. We usually choose it to keep away the feelings underneath till we are prepared to face them. It may perhaps feel like all-consuming, but provided that it does not consume you for a lengthy period of time, it is part of your emotional management. It is a valuable emotion until you have progressed past the first waves of it. Then you'll be prepared to go deeper. In the course of grief and grieving you'll have numerous subsequent visits with anger in its various forms. Beneath anger is pain, your pain. It's natural to experience a feeling of abandonment, but we dwell in a society that fears annoyance. People usually tell us our anger is inappropriate. Several people may look at your anger as being harsh. Unluckily for them, they too will tell the anger of loss sooner or later. But at the moment, your crucial task is to honor your anger by letting yourself to be angry. Scream if you there is need to. Find a private place and let it out.

Anger is a strong point and it can be an anchor, providing temporary framework to the nothingness of loss. At first, grief seems as being lost at sea: with no link to anything. Then you start being mad at someone, maybe a person who wasn't present at the funeral, maybe an individual who is not around, perhaps a person who has changed now that your loved one has passed away. Abruptly you have a framework—your resentment towards them. The anger acts like a bridge over the open sea, a link from you to them. It a thing to hold on to, and a network made from the power of anger feels better than nothing.

BARGAINING

Before a death of your loved one, you can be willing to do anything if only your dear one may be given another chance.

After a loss, this type of stage may take the form of a short-term truce. "What if I dedicate the rest of my life to assisting others? Then can I wake and recognize this has all been a terrible dream?

We would like life delivered what it was, we would like our cherished one restored. We would like to return back in time: to find a tumor early, identify the disease more rapidly, stop the accident from. Guilt is most often bargaining's companion. If they only cause us to find problem with yourself and what we think, we could have done differently. We can even bargain with pain. We'll do something not to feel the pain of this loss. We stay static in the past, attempting negotiate our way out from the hurt.

In other cases, bargaining might help our brain move in one state of loss to another. It may be a way station which gives our mind the time it might need to adjust. Bargaining might fill the gaps which our strong emotions usually dominate, which frequently keep suffering far away. It enables us to believe we may bring order to chaos which has taken over and it changes with time. We might start out bargaining for the cherished one to be saved. Later, we might even bargain that we may die rather than our cherished one. Whenever we accept that they're going to die we can bargain that their demise may be painless.

Following a death, bargaining frequently is moving from the past into the future. We might bargain that we'll see our family members again in heaven. We might bargain and ask for a respite from diseases in our household, or that no additional disasters visit our family members. A mother who drops a young kid might bargain that her other kids remain safe and healthy. Eric Clapton, well recognized for his song "Tears in Heaven" creates about his youthful son who fell unfortunately to his death. A few of the lyrics might be interpreted as the negotiating stage, when he wondered whether he'll stop crying when he eventually gets to paradise.

As we undertake the negotiating procedure, the mind changes past occasions while discovering those what if, and if only, statements. Sadly, the mind unavoidably comes to the same conclusion. The tragic the truth is that our cherished one is really gone.

DEPRESSION

After negotiating, our interest goes directly into the present. This depressive phase seems as though it'll last forever. It is critical to realize that this depression isn't a sign of mental illness. We pull away from life, left in a haze of intense sadness, questioning, maybe, if there's any stage in going on alone.

After a loss of a person closest to you, you are engulfed with depression, and is usually seen as unusual condition. Are you in a depressing condition? It is a crucial question you should ask yourself. The loss of a person close to you is a very depressing state, and depression is a common, normal and right response. When you don't experience depression once a loved one dies would be strange. When a loss completely settles in your soul, the understanding that your loved one did not get better this time and isn't coming back is reasonably depressing.

ACCEPTANCE

Acceptance is usually confused with the view of being satisfied with what has happened. This isn't the case. Most individuals do not ever feel okay and sound about the loss of a person they loved. In this stage it is about accepting the true outcome that our person we love is physically gone and realizing that this new actuality is the indefinite reality. We will at no time like this reality or make it satisfactory, but finally we accept it. We get used to live with it. It is the new usual thing with which we must get used to. This is where our ultimate healing and alteration can take a firm hold, even though the fact that healing usually looks and seems to be an unattainable condition. Finding acceptance may perhaps be like having more good days than terrible ones. As we start living again and enjoy our life, we usually feel that in doing so, we are forsaking or betraying those people we loved. We can never take back what has been lost, however we can make new networks, new meaningful relationships, fresh and new interdependencies. Rather than denying our feelings, we pay attention to our needs; we move, we transform, we grow, we progress. We may begin reaching out to others and involve ourselves in their lives. We advance in our friendships and in our relationship together. We start living again, but we can't do so till we have given grief its deserved time.

Not everyone who is grieving will experience each of these stages, and you don't have to go through each stage of the process to heal. Emotions and feelings are messy and can't be stuffed into neat boxes, so don't worry about what you think you "should" be feeling at any given time. Some people may experience none of these stages, or there may be other emotions that an individual experiences that aren't listed here. It is a cyclical journey and can manifest in many ways.

Loss and Transition

Even if our loss is anticipated or planned for, it tosses us into a place of uncertainty. It's a time of change, and for a lot of people, change can make them very anxious. The un- known is sometimes a worrying and frustrating place to be.

We are dealing with a void left by the loss, and a disruption of our focus and routines. It means we will have to enter a period of transition, restructuring, and rethinking. We will have to reorganize our lives in a different way to accommodate the loss, and that can be a major upheaval.

We'll need to find something else to fill the gap, even though it will not replace a loved one, and also begin to understand that they will now be with us in other, non-physical ways.

Love can help to heal the pain of grief and bring meaning back into our lives, whether it's self-love, the love of a person or animal, the love of a new interest or job, or something else.

Eventually, we will heal, but it will take time to reminisce, reflect, allow and explore healthy expression of what we are thinking and feeling, and to focus on the journey of how we can piece ourselves back together. Grief can help to create fertility in our lives, where new loves and possibilities can grow. With loss often comes a journey of discovery, personal growth, and profound wisdom, and we can allow ourselves to heal by turning our pain into something meaningful.

Allowing Yourself Space to Grieve

One of the problems of our modern society is that we often don't have the space we need to grieve. We're uncomfortable with loss in general. It reminds us that even humans have limitations – that there are aspects of our life that we're not in control of. It bursts our bubble and let's us know that we're vulnerable, particularly where the death of a loved one (human or animal) is concerned. This is one part of life that can't be avoided after we involve ourselves in a relationship with someone. This makes us encounter loss and grief.

We'd rather not be reminded of something painful in our lives, and are often told, "Don't worry, you'll be OK" ; "Just try and get on with your life" ; "Everything will work out all right". We're taught that we have to put a brave face on things and tough it out! Some people will try and avoid those who are grieving all together, rather than have to talk to them, either because they're unsure how to approach the subject (should they talk about the loss or not?), or because they find the subject distasteful or upsetting. Either way, society would rather we just hurry up and get back to normal again, but this kind of message actually does nothing to help us deal with our grief because it puts too much pressure on us. Trying to ignore or suppress our grief will only make it worse in the long run, and can lead to depression, substance abuse, anxiety, and health problems. Unreleased pain can turn your heart into a toxic wound that doesn't heal.

Loss makes us what we are: human beings. When we suffer loss, we grieve, and there's no getting away from it, however uncomfortable it makes us. It's natural and healthy for us to grieve; to acknowledge our pain and accept it is part of the recovery journey. The most important thing we can do is allow ourselves the time and space to go through our own sacred healing. Be patient, treat yourself gently, and just be.

The intended meaning of this Book is to help:

- It aids you to have the knowledge of exhibiting the feelings of rage, panic, being unhappy and also being uneasy. This encourages you to move on life after loss.
- Also aids you see the better side of the loss.
- set aside time to the grief process and its expression
- Explore positive ways of dealing with your loss
- Let you realize that you are not alone

During grief and loss, meditations are also incorporated. It helps in generating constructive and optimistic practices in our lives as well as making it easy for our recovery. In addition, we regain back our morale, composure and making us trust ourselves once again. Looking after ourselves mentally and practicing self-love and self-nurture is an important, and often overlooked, part of overcoming grief and loss, and maintaining our physical health.

CHAPTER 03
EMBRACING YOUR FEELINGS

At this stage of your grief journey, you may have begun to accept the concept that grief is a normal and necessary part of healing after loss. Perhaps you have also come to under- stand that expressing your feelings is a natural and critical component of grieving. But what if, most of the time, you find yourself not feeling any particular emotion—no sadness, no anxiety, no anger? Mostly you just experience yourself as being numb. What do you do?

First, keep in mind that it does not help to judge your grief experience. Being numb much of the time is just what is happening right now. It is not wrong. You have not sabotaged all possibilities for healing and rediscovering the goodness in life. Having this attitude of acceptance will allow you room to make new choices without blaming yourself for "not doing it right."

Next, understand that numbness can have its place in the grief journey. In fact, it is normal to go numb in the early days after suffering a loss. Numbness can protect you from being engulfed or overwhelmed with extreme sadness or fear. Soon after the death of a loved one, for example, it is not at all unusual to "zone out" during the funeral or memorial service. The feelings at that moment may simply be too much to take on, whereas they may crop up often in the next few days or weeks.

You may have a similar experience if your loss involves a medical crisis—when the doctor gives you the bad news, or the surgery is incomplete—and you just feel numb. If this happens to you, do not be upset if someone misinterprets your actions. "I just cannot grasp how you can just sit there through the whole funeral with that void appearance?" a kinfolk member or colleague may claim, with the implication being that somehow you do not care enough about the beloved or that you were being disrespectful. Remember that you were simply taking care of yourself. Your numbness formed a protective shield.

You may notice that you go numb after you have just begun to feel an intense emotion. The tears start to flow, and they just keep pouring out for several minutes. You may get panicky, fearful that they won't stop and you will not be able to regain control of yourself and your actions. You stuff the feeling back inside. Going numb is a "flight" response to escape the torrent of tears.

This, too, can be a normal part of the grief process, for a while. The problem emerges if numbness prevails as your most frequent state of being and your feelings remain mostly submerged for weeks, months, or even years. That problem can become magnified if you encourage the numbness response by turning to a crutch, such as drinking alcohol in excess or watching mindless TV programs for hours, day after day. Behaviors like these push you further and further away from the feelings that are waiting to be expressed. Conversely, when you make the choice to stay open to your feelings and find safe ways to fully experience them—as often as you need to and for as long as necessary each time—you are taking a positive step in your grief journey.

Just as continually going around in a state of numbness can block your healing, so too can pretending that you must be "okay" because you are not having strong emotions. You might say to yourself and to those who care about you, "I'm not crying all the time. I'm not screaming in anger or agony. I don't have a problem with grief. I don't need help." In reality, you may simply be avoiding the natural expression of those feelings, an expression that will help you gradually to feel better instead of remaining seemingly okay.

You may find yourself afraid of feeling your emotions, because you are just not used to doing so. You have always been in control, keeping your head on straight so you can do your job and function effectively in your life. Choosing to express your feelings can be a big change.

Making room for your feelings may require tuning out some of the standards or beliefs that come from the outside.

You may need to reject the outmoded, conventional concepts that "fragile men are the simply ones who cry," or that "big girls do not cry." In reality, crying, and every other emotional expression, is natural responses to painful loss for any human being. It is actually a sign of strength.

You may need to overcome other misguided beliefs and habits held by your family, such as pretending that emotions are not real or are to be avoided in the name of staying sane or rational. It may be necessary to reevaluate influences of your culture or environment that could discourage you from allowing your feelings to have their place.

Once you adopt a more accepting attitude toward your feelings, they will naturally begin to show up more regularly. Still, you may find yourself afraid that the feelings triggered by your grief will just be too much to handle and will take you too far from your comfort zone. If you are prepared for the emotions that you are most likely to encounter, you will likely find them easier to deal with when they arrive.

EMBRACING YOUR FEELINGS

You may notice other feelings in your grief journey, or you may simply be feeling intense waves of the same emotion, such as sadness, again and again. That is natural. You may discover that your dominant emotion shifts after a period of time. You may progress from sadness to anger, for example. It is important to remember that emotions are unpredictable and sporadic. They can come upon you at any time, in any situation. A natural trigger for grief, such as opening the door to a deceased child's bedroom, may prompt deep wells of sadness to swirl up. But so can the seemingly most mundane and innocent moments.

Your feelings also do not certainly fit any certain design. That is true for the grief process itself. Remember, each person grieves differently. There is no right or wrong way.

Some theories about grief suggest that the grief journey can be marked by specific phases or stages. You may be familiar with what are often referred to as the five stages of grief. Those stages are: Denial, Anger, Bargaining, Depression and Acceptance.

The terrain of the grief journey has been described as covering a period of shock or denial, then an obsession with the loss, followed by a deeper despair, and then eventually recovery. Other grief specialists have pointed to just two basic stages: one, accepting the reality of the loss itself; and two, accepting the impact of the loss on your life and finding meaning in the experience of grieving and moving forward.

Another way to look at the process may be through the following phases:

1. Coming to terms with what happened.
2. Expressing and working through your feelings.
3. Changing to your "fresh normal" and discovering the individual you have turn out to be through the grief process.
4. Preparing for an enduring network with the person or life condition that you have lost.

As you become more and more comfortable with the idea of embracing your feelings and practicing other tools and strategies on the grief journey, you may find that one or more of these maps of the grief journey resonate with you. In that case, they may be helpful to you in providing a context for your experience as markers to find along the trail. However, your response to grief may not look like any of these models. In fact, your grief journey may not seem to be following any organized or logical progression or path at all.

Rather, it may take the form of a series of zigzags as you do your best to follow along. If that is happening for you, there is nothing wrong with your experience. You are simply reinforcing the reality that every grief journey is unique. Do not let anyone tell you how you should feel, or what state of grief you should be in, or what phase you need to enter next.

In fact, it can be harmful to try to force yourself to conform to some outlined system of dealing with a loss. It is entirely possible, for example, that you may never experience intense anger as part of any phase or period of grief. This does not mean you are failing to make progress, or that you have "skipped" a required step. If you are allowing yourself to have feelings, and your life is moving toward health and healing, do not worry about the absence of a particular emotion in your process. Do not allow any rigid outline of grief stages to become another "should" or a potential source of guilt if you do not follow it. Your feelings, and the grief journey itself, will take you where you need to go.

Making Room to Feel

What do you do if you have the intention to embrace your feelings but find that they are seldom showing up as you go through your day? You do not feel especially numb, and you are not aware of trying to suppress your emotions. But for one reason or another, your feelings just tend to be held at bay. Should you try to make them come out?

Again, grief is not about forcing anything. It is about accepting and allowing a natural process to unfold. However, because it is so very important to open up to your feelings, you may find it helpful to both allow and gently encourage their expression.

How? Let's say you have a vague sense that you are in- deed sad about the loss you have suffered, and you are aware that not allowing room for the sadness may slow your recovery. Here are ways you can allow your sadness a chance to raise to the surface:

- Look over some photos or other tangible reminders of your loved one. It may help to simply speak their name aloud a few times.
- Watch a terrible, sad, and familiar movie. If it made you cry before you suffered your loss, you may cry again now—and the tears this time may open the door to feeling the real sadness over your loss.
- Listen to some of your beloved's favorite songs, or perhaps songs that you enjoyed together. It may help to close your eyes briefly as you recall those moments of joy and union. Start a journal in which you record your day-to-day experiences since your loss. Then reflect back and write about those final days and hours before the loss and venture even further back to some special memories that you shared together.
- Sit for a few moments in quiet meditation or prayer.

Sometimes just taking a break from the business of life is enough to let the feelings in.

- Visit an Internet or in-person support group for those in grief, especially if you are likely to come across people there who have suffered a similar or comparable loss to yours. You may feel an urge to join in one of the discussion groups or other public postings, or you may choose to hold back and simply read and witness the sharing of others. It is quite possible that someone else's story will help you get access to your own emotions.

When you do decide to take an active step to make room for your feelings, take care to establish a safe space where you feel comfortable and are not likely to be disturbed. You may need to tell family members that you are visiting that safe place and need privacy for a while. After you have settled into your safe space, just sit for a few moments, breathe deeply, and gently explore whether a feeling may be arising. Let's say you have a vague notion that feelings of anger may be bubbling under the surface. Try this: Grab a pillow, and as you squeeze or hit it, focus on what might be making you angry. See if there are words that accompany this feeling: "You weren't supposed to ever leave me!" or it is not reasonable, you might choose instead to take out a piece of paper and use crayons or markers to draw an image of this anger.

As you begin to have positive experiences with letting your feelings come out, consider setting aside a specific time every day, or every other day, to return to your safe space.

You might continue to experiment with different approaches to allow or invite your feelings to emerge, or you may choose to just be quietly present and see what feelings arise. This will give you another opportunity to practice acceptance of any experience on your own unique grief journey.

As you become more open to the expression of your feelings, you may be surprised to find that you really do not fall apart. The world does not end. You still feel intact. This will give you confidence to continue to express even more feelings that may have been hidden.

Keep in mind, though, that you do not want to rush your expression of feelings. It is usually best to move slowly, giving yourself opportunities to explore and feel emotions related to your loss while still maintaining a balance in your life. You still need those occasions when your emotions are temporarily at rest. It is perfectly okay if you still find yourself wanting to spend some eras of time vegging out eyeing at the walls. The renovation now is that you know such behavior is temporary and that you have the skills and the tools to find the time and the means to embrace your feelings actively.

Notice that all of these options are steps that you can take by yourself. You may find that you are able to embrace your feelings and make valuable progress in your grief journey on your own. However, it is important to keep in mind that it is not wise to try to manage your entire grief process alone. For most of us, the full experience is simply too much. Additionally, there is so much to be gained from reaching out for the support of other people. These may include family and friends currently in your life, or new contacts on a similar journey who you make by seeking to connect with. The next chapter will discuss why reaching out to others is important and how you can successfully manage those relationships while grieving.

When you consider the pool of people who may be able to offer you support during your grief process, counselors or other health-care professionals are apt to have a prominent place on the list. In fact, you may find that turning to a professional for guidance and support may be a necessary step at some point in your grief journey. Before proceeding to the next chapter, it will be helpful to take an inventory of your current grief experience and consider whether it may be time to call upon a counselor for help right now.

Ten Signs That It May Be Time to Seek Professional Help with Your Grief

1) You have frequent bouts of hopelessness. While occasionally feeling hopeless about the future may be natural, if you find that it is happening more and more often, a counselor can help you explore such feelings in a safe way. If your hopeless feelings are leading you to indulge in alcohol or drug use, or if they are accompanied by suicidal thoughts, it is critical that you obtain help right away.

2) You spend considerable time searching for your departed loved one. It is natural to find yourself occasionally calling out for the one you have lost in a moment of temporarily forgetting what has happened.

But if you're frequently roaming your house or apartment actively searching for that person, and even expecting to find them there, that's something to share with an experienced counselor.

3) You lose an excessive amount of weight and become weak. It is natural to suffer some loss of appetite, but if your lack of eating continues for a prolonged period and results in significant weight loss, you will certainly want to be checked out by your doctor. A counselor can offer further assistance in helping you better manage your feelings and adopt healthier self-care strategies while the grief continues.

4) Your feelings of guilt become pervasive. If you find yourself obsessing over how this loss is all your fault to the point of pushing all other emotions aside, a counselor can help you see how you have become stuck and point you toward ways to find a better balance in your feelings and perspective.

5) You wish you had died instead of your beloved and you count the days until your death will come. Feeling lost or left behind when a loved one dies is natural and can trigger wonderment about why you did not die, too. However, if such feelings shift toward an active death wish, professional help is needed.

6) You notice alarming physical sensations, such as shortness of breath or slowed, slurred speech. This is another indicator that a medical checkup may be needed to rule out problems that extend beyond normal grief and require immediate attention.

7) You demonstrate an inability to perform simple daily tasks required for your basic well-being. This issue is especially important to deal with if you live alone.

Even if you live with family members who are willing to help pick up some of the pieces when you cannot function at your usual level, you may need to call upon outside support if you are so distraught and weak that you cannot dress or bathe yourself, or prepare food.

8) Your loss of appetite suddenly shifts to a pattern of overeating, which may be accompanied by nausea or vomiting. A counselor can help you sift through the emotional causes of your altered eating habits and prevent the pattern from getting worse.

9) You cannot trust anyone or anything, and you are constantly fighting with family members or others close to you. Yes, anger and frustration can often spill out unintentionally toward those who love us, especially if they tell us how we should feel or insist that we should "get over it." You can expect some strain or conflict in your relationships while in the midst of the grief process. However, you do not want the burden of constant conflict or the weight of thinking that no one can be trusted. A counselor can help you explore the feelings behind your attitude and suggest strategies for dealing with loved ones while taking care of yourself and the needs of your grief. For a time, you may believe that things have really been clicking in your management of your grief journey. You are expressing your feelings. You are taking better care of yourself. You discover the proverbial light towards the end of the tunnel. Then you suffer a setback that leaves you dispirited and insecure about what to do or where to go. A counselor can help shine a light on what happened and guide you to discover new possibilities for continuing on your grief journey.

Even if you decide that your needs are not that acute, you may want to begin seeing a counselor just so you have someone to talk to. If you do choose to seek out a counselor, it is important to find someone who understands the grief journey. Track down the names of professionals in your community who may specialize in grief counseling or who have extensive experience in guiding those like you who have suffered a major loss.

Interview any potential counselor and make sure that person's beliefs and attitudes about grief are in alignment with your own. This is an important partnership, one that can significantly propel you forward on your grief journey.

CHAPTER 04
MANAGEMENT OF GRIEF/DISTRESS

Ten Steps to Healing a Broken Heart

Losing a loved one is devastating. There are no shortcuts to fixing a broken heart. Grief is a process that you have to go through in order to get complete healing. While things may never be the same again, you can still come back from the heartbreak and live your life again.

So to help you get on the right track, here are ten steps to complete healing:

1. Admit that you're in a crisis. Admit that you are hurting and it is okay to not be okay; it is actually normal in times like these. You shouldn't isolate yourself from your friends and family. The best way to recover is to spend time with them, even if you feel like being alone.

2. Accept the pain. As mentioned in the previous chapter, embrace grief, for you cannot hide from it anyway. Reality bites! People get heartbroken. If your loved one dies, it is something that you have to accept. Remember that nothing is permanent in this world. Losing something that mattered to you can be painful. Acceptance is an integral factor in your healing process.

3. Change your thoughts. The death of a loved one can be destructive. This could be the best time to change your frame of mind and look at things from a different perspective. You have to learn to bounce back from each fall. Look at the loss as an opportunity to find some time for yourself or to find a new career path.

4. Learn to understand what you're feeling. Get in touch with your emotions to better understand them. The feeling of extreme pain and sadness will never go away if you don't deal with them. The sooner you deal with them, the better you understand them. Go through the process. Feel the anger, the resentment, feel the pain, and feel the fear, even the shame. Take them all in. Once you've understood them, it will be easier to accept your loss.

5. Believe that you deserve to be happy. If you have lost a loved one, do not pity yourself; instead take this opportunity to improve yourself. Take some time off and just be happy.

Death is more difficult to accept because the loved one is gone forever but you have to face the music; you are still alive, so make your life matter.

6. Learn some new things. Take up a new hobby or a sport. When your mind is occupied, you have less time to feel sorry for yourself. Keep yourself occupied. The moment you become reclusive, it will take longer for you to recover.

7. Keep a journal so you can write about what you feel. You'll be surprised to find out how writing about what you feel helps you to talk to your own self. By writing them all out, you will begin to understand what you feel. Instead of venting your anger or sadness on other people, better channel them in a constructive way. When the most difficult times are over and you read them back, you'll be able to gain new insights. You'll learn how you were able to get past that difficult part of your life.

8. Try to connect with the community. Do volunteer works. The key is to not feel alone. Pain when shared with those who are in the same situation will be easier to bear.

9. Go on a vacation. Is there a place where you'd like to visit? If your parents live across the country, now is the best time to be with them.

You might have lost your one great love to death but that doesn't mean you cannot fall in love again. Consider the possibility of falling in love again. While you shouldn't force yourself to do so, it doesn't hurt to consider it as an option after a few years. Concentrate on yourself first and your journey to recovery. When the time is right it will happen.

An analogy of physiological disease might be helpful. The Centers for Disease Control define disease as the absence of effective antibodies, not the presence of a toxic environment. This suggests increasing our ability (emotional "antibodies") to manage poignant grief is more effective than attempting to minimize or ignore it.

Initially, walk toward the pain for gradual desensitization. Confront emotional pain by accepting it. It is healthy and okay to cry. Tears help relieve distress. Trying to be macho by concealing or ignoring grief is ineffective and will merely prolong it.

After emotions stabilize, talk about what bothers you. This can be difficult but it helps to flush out pain. By doing so you are likely to eat better, sleep better, remain healthier, and reduce disruption in your home and work life.

For example, what will you miss the most about your loved one? What is the worst thing about this for you now? Talk about these things repeatedly for desensitization, and let family and friends know you need to do this.

The ability to talk about it indicates the ability to manage it. The more you talk about your loved one the easier it becomes. That's the goal! It's that simple. If previous experiences are affecting you now, bring them up also. They too need to be resolved for a better present life.

Regular physical activity such as brisk walking, aerobics, swimming, bicycling, and some deep breathing, help to cope with distress. Alternate, exercise with relaxation, and mourning with happy times. Balance is a key word in life.

Pause to enjoy simple contemplative pleasures—"smell the roses." Listen to music, read a book, go to a concert or ball game, and enjoy life. Finding happiness reduces hypertension and is heart healthy. Isn't that what your loved one would desire for you?

Love continues existing on as you move on. Put an end to unhealthy activities such as smoking, abuse of drugs, binge taking and/or binge drinking, not physically exercising, or spending too much time on the computer and Internet, or over watching TV. A big mistake is trying to subdue sorrows with alcohol. It will have the opposite effect! When you are depressed, alcohol becomes a depressant. When the momentary blur wears off, you will feel much worse. Never use alcohol to medicate emotional distress. It's like pouring gasoline on a fire.

What about prescribed mood medication? If a medical condition is causing or contributing to depression, then medication may be in order. This can require differential diagnosis to determine if depressive bereavement is circumstantial and/or medical. Medical causes include drugs, alcohol, environmental toxins, infections, sever hyperthyroidism, a chemical imbalance in the brain, anemia, and anoxia. An indication of medical causation is that some of the same symptoms existed prior to your loss.

Meds may be needed in the short term if you are experiencing extreme complicated grief. Evidence is lacking, however, to suggest the use of meds for normal bereavement.

Avoid suppressing grief. To get through it, it is necessary to go through it. Medication is a chemical pathway to feeling restored. "Happy pills" don't cope with underlying causation and thus can impede real emotional recovery and prolong the grief process. Meds may also have unpleasant side effects and become addictive.

From time to time you may find solace in talking to the decedent even though you do not receive an audible response. Whether this is fantasy or the decedent really hears you, we simply don't know. Someday on the other side we will gain an understanding of "paranormal activity." In the meantime, if it provides comfort and a sense of presence, do it.

Traumatic and treasured memories do not erode like every day memories. As the frequency and severity of emotional pain diminishes over time, your loved one and the past will be preserved in your thoughts. You may occasionally re- experience your loss by unpleasant imaginably intrusion. Avoid addiction to this. Focus on pleasant endearing memories.

Precious memories can help sustain you through rough emotional terrain and make you a stronger, better person. For years, things like holidays, anniversaries, birthdays, or just talking about him or her may trigger treasured memories—like having roses in December.

You may hesitate to say goodbye to grief after it has become familiar to you, or because it might seem like you are abandoning your loved one. Don't fall in love with sorrow or build a shrine to grief. Ultimately, humor and self-care are needed.

At some point allow yourself to arrive at the end of your painful journey so you can begin the rest of your life. Let the darkness become light. Accepting the finality of your loved one's death is not forgetting your loved one. Completed grief is when you can think about your loved one with peace instead of pain.

Self-Care of Emotions

Emotional trauma needs relationships—not just dogma—to heal. Like the final resting place for raindrops, the final resting place for emotional trauma is in the community. On the other hand, there are helpful things you can do for yourself.

Only you can determine the pace and extent of emotional withdrawal from the deceased. Some remain emotionally connected; others eventually let go in order to move on.

There is not necessarily a right or wrong. Past painful experiences can intrude into the present as perceived threats. There is no inoculation for this. However, there are things you can do to facilitate relaxation and serenity.

For example, if you want to relax in the presence of emotional stressors, relax your pelvic floor muscles, the muscles that surround the bones you sit on. Don't flex and squeeze your buttocks together like you instinctively would if suddenly alarmed or tensed. Let them be totally unclenched and limp. This interacts with your central nervous system helping your body to relax.

It is a technique used in sports such as football. When a well-trained quarterback takes a snap, drops back to pass without finding an open receiver, sees a 300 pound tackle coming full speed at him and knows he's going to get hit, what does he do? If he tenses and braces for the hit, he is apt to get hurt and possibly injured, instead, he relaxes his pelvic floor muscles and lets his body become limp. Bruises may appear, but injury is unlikely. He gets up prepared for the next snap.

Resiliency and relaxation go hand-in-hand. We've all heard stories of the drunk who survives a horrible auto accident, uninjured, that might have killed someone else. Now you know why.

When confronted by stressors, other relaxing techniques while softening your pelvic floor muscles include folding your hands behind your head, pulling your elbows back to stretch your chest, and breathing deeply.

Also try humming simple familiar tunes like, "Happy Birthday" or a favorite hymn. This may seem silly, but try it! Momentarily disconnect from life's activities. I like to hum "Amazing Grace."

Grief and Loss

Twenty-Five Best Coping Practices

There's an old saying that, "If we keep doing what we're doing, we'll keep getting what we are getting." Select those practices you are ready for now—not too many at one time.

Take it one day at a time. Be positive and avoid excuses. Be patient, but keep nudging yourself along. Counseling may help more than you imagine.

1. Walk toward the pain. Don't subdue it; go through it. It's the only way out. Ignoring or masking the grief prolongs the pain.

2. Avoid trying to be macho. Concealing reality restrains recovery.

3. Crying is healthy and okay. Let your feelings show honestly.

4. Don't be in a hurry to remove your loved one's belongings. They can provide a sense of presence. Don't allow others to control this.

5. Keep and organize your loved one's photos, videos, and other endearing mementos.

6. Journalize your thoughts, emotions, and reactions. This becomes therapeutic when you share it with others.

7. Sometimes it is comforting to talk to your loved one even though there is no audible response. It can provide a sense of presence. What would your loved one say to you now if he or she were your counselor and comforter?

8. Occasionally compose a letter to your loved one. These can be memorable keepsakes.

9. Rituals such as lighting a candle or planting a memorial tree can be comforting reminders.

10. Take care of yourself physically. Get enough sleep and eat nutritious meals high in carbohydrates and low in sugar.

11. Avoid excessive use of caffeine—a blood pressure elevator.

MANAGEMENT OF GRIEF/DISTRESS

12. Don't use alcohol or not prescribed drugs to medicate emotional pain! When depressed, drugs and alcohol act as depressants. They may provide a momentary blur, but then depression shall return with a vengeance!

13. Exercise. Aerobics and walking are excellent to help manage adrenalin.

14. Forgive yourself for all the things you believe you should have said or done. Avoid critiquing and blaming yourself.

15. Forgive your loved one for any conflicts that existed.

16. Avoid feeling guilty that you are still alive.

17. Avoid isolation, especially being alone on holidays, birthdays, anniversaries, and other special days for a while.

18. Spend time with others. Let them know you appreciate their support.

19. Tell and retell what is bothering you the most until it is no longer bothering you the most.

20. Get help and accept offered help. People do care and want to help.

21. Put off major life changing decisions for at least a year if possible.

22. Keep busy and focused. Idleness can produce morbidity.

23. Indulge yourself by doing things you enjoy—get out and have fun. Reignite a sense of humor and happiness!

24. Welcome back a sense of purpose. Reevaluate your life and invest in it. Take hold of the future and reassess your goals and plans. Start with small goals and work your way up. Your experience should reach a positive turning point. It's not too late to seek a better world.

25. Remember with love instead of pain; take hold of peace and a new life gain. Love lasts beyond grief through a commitment to living again. It's okay to be happy, and this honors your loved one. Death ends a life but not necessarily a relationship. There is a sense in which your loved one remains with you. Reframe your life. Let the new epoch begin! The term epoch is

employed deliberately. It means more than simply a period of time. It is a period of time marked by some- thing uniquely or highly significant—a memorable development.

CHAPTER 05
REBUILDING YOUR ROUTINE

The analogy of feeling as if your world has been pulled out from under you has been used in this book to describe the sensations that can occur after suffering a major loss. It is natural that your daily routine will be drastically shaken up as well. As discussed, you may find it difficult to eat regularly, sleep through the night, or to get up on time in the morning.

Basic personal hygiene may seem unimportant, or, conversely, something to obsess about as a way to avoid facing your feelings. Resuming your work schedule or the responsibilities of taking care of your children and your home can seem overwhelming. The challenge of managing your finances looms as well, especially if your loss has taken the form of the death of a spouse or a parent, and created a whole new set of money concerns.

Your grief is likely taking its toll on your physical health as well. You may be losing weight and experiencing gastrointestinal distress. Or you are battling fatigue or suffering new aches and pains. You may be more prone to colds and other illnesses, or might just look pale most of the time.

If health-related or other personal issues had occurred before you entered into a period of grieving, you likely would have followed the needed steps to take care of yourself and regain your normal, healthy state. However, when grief has taken a hold, you may lack the energy or the inclination to pay proper attention to such needs. You may find yourself saying, "What does it matter?" The loss itself, and the sadness that has enveloped you, seems to have completely taken over your life. Nothing else appears worthy of your attention. And yet, as your loved ones and your doctor may be reminding you, taking care of yourself physically and becoming active again does matter. In fact, doing so is an essential part of managing your grief, just as much a part of healing as learning to embrace your feelings and reaching out to others for emotional support.

So how do you address these physical and practical needs?

The answer is: the same way you approach your other needs in the grief process. This means calling upon patience and flexibility, and remembering that your grief journey is unique and does not follow a straight line. In other words, there is no one definite way to start taking better care of yourself and begin to rebuild your routine; there is only the way that will be right for you. In this chapter, you will find tools and strategies to help you get a handle on this part of your grief process. These methods will point you in the right direction, but ultimately you will be creating a plan that best fits who you are and how you are responding to your loss.

Use the ideas and tips that follow to begin reclaiming your healthy routine.

Four Tips to Help with Changed Sleep Habits

1. Try to get up at the same time each morning. You may find yourself going to bed much later than usual or waking up frequently during the night. This may lead to getting up later than you used to. That is okay, if you are able to accommodate the change into your schedule and responsibilities, but it may be helpful to get up about the same time each day so that you start to re-establish a new routine. For instance, if you were used to wake up at 6 a.m., maybe you can now plan on getting up at 7:30 a.m. and begin your day with a few moments of meditation or deep breathing exercises.

2. Schedule regular naps. If you lost a lot of sleep during a restless night, a brief nap can help you maintain your energy and strength. Even if you do not sleep during the time you designate for a nap, just resting and closing your eyes can be helpful.

3. Take a bath before going to bed. For many people, this is a reliable way to reduce stress and prepare for sleep.

While grieving, you are exposed to absentmindedness and may not remember about simple activities. Remember to consider this nightly bath as part of your grief routine. Listen to soothing music as part of your nighttime routine. If you are suffering the loss of a loved one, the late hours of the night are not usually the best time to bring out the favorite songs you used to share with your beloved. Instead, choose relaxing music to help soothe your nerves and let you drift closer to sleep.

4. Keep a journal and night light near your bed as tools to let you process feelings that may be keeping you awake. When grief has triggered bouts of insomnia, it is easy to fall into a pattern of just lying awake in bed mulling over the same thoughts of hopelessness or despair. Doing so is not usually helpful in getting back to sleep. If you instead reach for your journal to write down what you are thinking and feeling, the act of expressing those disturbing thoughts and images may encourage them to recede, which may help relax your mind enough to sleep. You may note a useful insight or idea that you can reexamine in the light of day and consider how to put it to use in your grief process.

Having a journal nearby provides the opportunity to write down the details of any dream that has awakened you from your sleep. Later, you may wish to reflect on any aspects of your dream that may be helpful, such as a clearer understanding of certain feelings or even a "message" that you can apply to your daily life.

Five Tips to Help with Changed Eating Habits

1. Eat small, healthy snacks. You may find that you are only able to eat one regular meal a day, or maybe not even that. While grieving, it usually does not help to try to force yourself to sit down at regular mealtimes and have some kind of breakfast, lunch, or dinner. Nevertheless, you need to preserve your strength.

Small, healthy snacks, such as fruit, yogurt, or nuts can help. You will know the healthy foods that your body likes best. You might consider protein shakes, energy bars, or supplements, but a consultation with your doctor may be helpful in sorting out the pros and cons of any meal substitutes. Natural foods are generally best for you, so try to eat these kinds of snacks at least a few times a day. Even a little at a time helps.

2. Consider accepting an invitation from family or friends to go out to lunch or dinner. For some people who are grieving, eating at home may be more difficult than eating out, especially if you have lost a loved one with whom you shared your home. A change of scenery may be enough to encourage you to at least try a cup of soup, nibble on a salad, or eat some bread and cheese. At the very least, having someone's company during the meal hour may take your mind off your suffering, at least for a while.

3. Avoid unhealthy foods. Staying away from alcohol and drugs is critical in maintaining basic health during grief, of course, but it is also important to refrain from junk food as your only source of nutrition for the day.

Keep in mind that the urge for unhealthy foods while suffering a major loss is most likely a sign of emotional distress. See if you can practice safe ways of expressing your feelings instead of devouring candy bars.

4. Drink plenty of water as well as healthy beverages, such as natural fruit juices and caffeine-free teas. Dehydration becomes more of a threat when you are not eating regularly. Keep a bottle of water with you as you go around your house or at work. Juices and teas can provide further sustenance. Coffee with its caffeine, though temporarily comforting, will not help you manage your stress.

5. Spend a little time preparing a favorite dish or meal, and then offer it to someone who cares about you. First, this gesture can be an excellent way of showing your gratitude for family or friends who are assisting you with practical or emotional support during your grief. The payoff is that you might be tempted to sample some of what you have made yourself!

Five Tips to Help with Daily Tasks and Responsibilities

1. Do not be afraid to ask for help. Remember, the people who love you usually want to help. Many are reluctant to approach you, however, either because they are anxious about witnessing your emotional distress or they do not know how to help you. So, if you are having problems keeping up with basic household tasks or errands, call upon someone close to you to handle specific tasks. Not only will it help get things done, it may also open a door to greater closeness with the person you have entrusted with balancing your check-book or walking your dog. You may want to ask a friend to serve as your designated contact person, someone with whom you can simply check in once a day to let them know that you are all right as well as get important messages or make sure that no emergency has arisen.

2. Make checklists of the most important daily and weekly tasks that need attention. Many things that you normally do as part of your daily routine just do not seem to be getting done while you are grieving, and in your current state you may struggle to even remember what those minor tasks are. It is helpful to make checklists to help focus on your everyday needs: sorting the mail, doing the laundry, starting and emptying the dishwasher, responding to emails, and so forth. For each item on the checklist, make notes about whether the task has been completed today, assigned to a helper, or postponed for a specific later time.

3. Do not feel obligated to answer every e-mail or phone message. Those who have suffered a recent loss are often overwhelmed by the number of expressions of caring and support that come pouring in every day, along with questions about their physical and emotional state. If that happens, trying to keep up with those messages can drain your energy and trigger surges of emotion that you are not prepared to cope with now. Give yourself permission to put on hold the act of responding to those contacts. It may help to put a standing message on your voice mail or inbox that explains your situation and respectfully asks for the understanding of loved ones if you do not get back to them for a while. A friend who has stepped in to help with daily tasks could perhaps be enlisted to assist you in prioritizing messages and forwarding responses in your name.

4. Be aware of particular tasks or activities that may trigger your grief. Going through the belongings of a loved one who has passed away will take time as well as an understanding of the emotional impact on you. Do not rush yourself.

5. Be honest and clear about communicating your needs and your limits. Be honest with yourself about what you are ready and able to handle at any particular period in your grief process. Then, tell others who are involved. If you have a job, talk to your supervisor or employer to fill them in as much as appropriate about your experience and negotiate any changes needed in your workload or schedule to help you stay on track with your grief process. Make clear to them that this is a priority! At home, talk to your spouse or other family members about what you honestly feel you can and cannot do in regard to your usual tasks and responsibilities. Emphasize that you need time to grieve. Help strategize with them about how to fill in the gaps.

Merits of exercising when grieving

The Need to Exercise No matter how well you are doing with your eating, sleeping, and daily tasks and activities, it is critical to engage in at least some physical exercise. You of course know that exercise helps to reduce stress, and you have learned how the stress from a major loss can have significant effects physically and emotionally. Physical exercise can help keep your grief from advancing to a state of depression. Whether or not you previously followed any kind of exercise routine, it is important to get active now.

Of course, like many positive goals, this one may seem beyond your grasp at times when grief takes hold. You're tired, you're sad; you're not feeling positive about your life and your future. Exercise may seem like the last thing you would want to do. So how do you summon the energy and the will to exercise, even a little? It helps just to start somewhere and discover for yourself what will encourage you to follow up with more regular physical activity. Here are some ideas for starting points:

• Take a short walk. Even if you walk for as little as five minutes, near your home or office is helpful in getting your body loosened up, as well as breathing in some fresh air. If you do it once, see if you can commit to walking for five minutes twice a week, Try to progress to three times a week. Once you find a pace that you are comfortable with, stick with it for a while and try to make it a part of your regular routine. You can always expand on it, as you feel stronger and more engaged in life.

If you struggle to walk for five minutes, start smaller. Is your mailbox located at the end of a long driveway or down one or more flights of stairs? Assign yourself the activity of walking to get the mail every day. Then try to move on from there.

- Try dancing. If you already enjoy dancing, this wonderful form of exercise may be a natural outlet during grief. Even if you have not done much dancing for years, or ever at all, you may find that it is something that fits in your adjusted daily routine now. You do not need to leave home to get started. Just put on some music that you sense will encourage you to start moving your body. Close your eyes if you wish.

Do not be concerned with how you look, or how slow and awkward your movements may appear at first. You are not performing, and no one is watching. You are just trying to get your body loosened up. And you just may find that it frees up some of the pressure in your mind as well.

- Go for a bike ride. As with dancing, it does not matter whether or not biking was a part of your fitness routine before you suffered your loss. Just get out and try riding around your backyard or your driveway or a short distance down the road. If you successfully bike for a few minutes one day, try to repeat the activity the next day before inviting yourself to go a little further.

As with walking, being outside will also help clear your head.

- Do yoga. If you have enjoyed attending yoga classes in the past, you may try to reclaim that outlet, staying for only as long as you feel comfortable. However, if you do not feel ready to be around others, or you are new to yoga, you can start with an instructional video or online workout program and practice at home. The stretching exercises will help alleviate stress.

- Get out in nature and explore physical ways to express your feelings. Just being in the woods or by a lake or stream can lessen some of your stress. You do not have to go far or map out a strenuous hike. Driving to a familiar and easily accessible nature spot is fine.

Once you are there, see what your instincts tell you to do. You might walk around the scenic area for a few moments, for example. If you are feeling angry and frustrated, perhaps you will benefit from throwing rocks in the water or safely pounding a stick against a boulder. That is good exercise!

- Visit a gym or fitness center. If you already belong to a fitness center, you may have stopped going because you are feeling too self-conscious or you just do not have the energy. Perhaps now you can convince yourself to go back with the reassurance that you will not try to plunge right into any previous workout routine.

Instead, try doing only a small portion of your usual regimen. Rather than going two or three times a week, start with once a week. See what your capability is and how it may expand over time. If you do not belong to a fitness center, see if you can set up a trial membership. Go at least a few times and experiment with different ways to engage your body again.

- Do some gardening. Whether you happen to be an avid gardener or have not spent time tending to plants or vegetables for years, consider beginning or re-establishing some kind of garden in your yard if you have one, or on your patio, terrace, or balcony. If it is not practical or beyond your scope to plant a garden of your own, ask a friend, neighbor, or family member who has a garden if you can help out there for a little while. If it has been a while since you have done any gardening, you may have forgotten how much exercise you get with all the bending, digging, lifting, and moving dirt around.

There are many other ways to get physically active, and with very little effort, you are likely to find what will work best for you. If you have young children or there are young children in your extended family or circle of friends, volunteer to visit with them for a little while. They will almost certainly get you moving again!

CHAPTER 06
TURNING LOSS INTO HEALING

When a loved one dies, we have lost someone external to ourselves. We think our lives will forever be incomplete. We allow ourselves to believe that our inner happiness and our capacity to love are dependent on individuals and circumstances we have no ability to control. But the route through the sadness is to dive deeper into our own hearts, our own souls, and our own intuitive trust.

Loss enters our lives in a variety of ways. Some losses come suddenly, unexpectedly, with no chance to prepare, not capable of even saying good-bye, no chance to say what was left unsaid or to do what was left undone.

Others losses come over time, perhaps through a prolonged illness, where numerous opportunities to have been set against a backdrop of physical and emotional suffering; the body and sometimes the mind of a loved one slowly deteriorate until they are no longer suitable vehicles to hold the being we loved. The relationship may end abruptly or linger on in a state of "near death" for years.

Because our culture has, historically, given us little valuable preparations for these unavoidable experiences, when a person closest to us dies we usually feel like we have crashed into a brick wall. We are totally confused and frustrated. We are shattered.

We are dazed. We keep replaying the facts in our minds, desperately searching for some misunderstanding, some mistake, and some missing piece that makes the actual thing emerges not to be real as we feel in our hearts it should be. The mind says, this just simply couldn't have happened. I can't imagine my life without...

And yet, when those we love have died or have left us, each morning we wake up and once again face the reality that they are physically gone. At times, we have to remind ourselves. It's as if we subconsciously hoped that the new dawn would bring a new reality, would rewrite history and erase the tragedy. If we have lost loved ones through death, we struggle to comprehend that which seems unthinkable, to expiate our horror that those we loved have chosen to leave us.

In either case, there are moments when we feel their presence within us. We hear their voice. We smell their perfume. We see them vividly in our mind's eye. We can almost feel their touch. We feel the way we would if they were here. But our intuitive, emotional sense of connection with them is at odds with our rational knowledge that they are gone. We are inclined to dismiss our sense of connection with them because we have no cultural context in which to understand it.

If we are working with a terminal disease in our own bodies, we have moments when we "forget" and, for whatever short period of time, we come out from under that dark cloud. And if we sense that we may have participated in the onset of the disease, as we might with certain forms of cancer, heart disease, cirrhosis, or AIDS, we face the guilt and confusion of having lived our lives with ambivalence. We question why we consciously engaged in behaviors that might have hastened life's end.

Each day we make decisions about how to deal with these realities. We may approach the pain and the confusion a little bit at a time, step-by-step as the days go by, responding to some deep intuitive understanding that our ability to live life fully will either be enhanced or diminished by the degree of honest awareness we can bring to these events.

We may notice that our cultural training, which has been to ignore, deny, and avoid whatever is unpleasant, leads us deeper into confusion and numbness by offering only distraction as a solution. We may also notice that the relentless effort of our minds to "understand" what has taken place in some refined way keeps the raw edge on our pain. We're caught in the agonizing misery of our grief because we frequently attempt to make use of our minds in resolving it, or to aid us ignore it. But the actual healing of grief cannot take place till we start the journey from the mind to the heart. And when the heart is broken, the thought of reentering it is terrifying. To be precisely, the healing occurs in the heart and when it is broken apart, it is as well left wide open.

Let's for instance, I tell you my readers a short story of my life during the grieving process. It has happened to me also and not only once but a several of times. For a period of five years, I have made it a practice to visit with, explore with, and at times care for people who are terminally ill. I also have spent a great deal of time intuitively navigating the sometimes stormy, sometimes fog-shrouded waters of grief—my own and that of many others. Often in the course of social conversation when I tell people that I spend time sitting at the bedsides of people who are dying and holding the hands of people in grief, the response is one of shock bordering on horror. "Oh my God! How do you do that? That must be so depressing!"

At an earlier time in my life, I would have reacted the same way. But at some point, because I had the opportunity to confront death so many times, I began to get the sense that in teaching us to avoid the unpleasant and encouraging us to deny the inevitable, our culture has robbed us of many, many precious opportunities to gain a deeper, more immediate sense of who we are and what our lives are all about.

We search desperately for meaning in life. We want to know that it all adds up to something, that we are not just random events in a trivial, uncaring, meaningless Universe. Intuitively, we sense that there must be something very profound about such an infinitely complex and intricate world.

But our cultural training encourages us to perceive the events of our lives and our world through a selective viewfinder. We always seek to filter out whatever is unpleasant. And yet, here it is inside us. And there it is around us.

By diverting our eyes, our minds, and our awareness from so much of what exists in our environment, by pretending that aging, decay, danger, and death are best dealt with through avoidance and ignorance, we have short-circuited our ability to fully experience what it is to be human. At the same time, we have cut off access to the parts of our beings that would be most helpful in times of emotional, spiritual, and existential crisis. We need only look at the widespread drug and alcohol abuse in our culture to realize that we are extremely unskilled at working with confusion, pain, and suffering. Most of us only know how to medicate and numb ourselves. We haven't got a clue about how to turn and face the demons that we think are tormenting us.

A number of years ago a friend of mine said to me, "If you want to get really high, try living in Truth." For a long time I pondered the meaning of that statement. And slowly, primarily through the frequent interaction with grief and dying, I began to see that Truth has extraordinary power. That looking directly at what is tremendously transformative. That every time we divert our eyes, every time we pretend that the people, places, and events of our lives are other than they are, we diminish our capacity to be whole beings. We subtly give ourselves the message that our hearts and minds are too small, too finite, too limited to handle the Universe and all of its infinite beauty and seemingly infinite horror.

So now I can share with you the certainty that dealing with grief and loss need not be depressing. In fact, it can be some of the most inspirational, uplifting, and meaningful work of a lifetime.

As Don Juan said to Carlos Casteneda in Journey to Ixtlan: Death is our eternal companion ... an immense amount of pettiness is dropped if your death makes a gesture to you, or if you just have the feeling that your companion is there watching you.

When a loved one has died, we are pushed beyond the boundaries our minds have created to maintain the illusion of safety, continuity, stability, and control. Our defenses crumble. We simply have no energy to support them. We are thrust into an uncomfortable realm of confusion and apprehension. The ways in which we have known and experienced our lives, our loved ones, and ourselves are in disarray.

It is—amazingly enough—an extremely ripe moment. It is a time when we have the opportunity to break free of the prisons in our minds that have held us back from fully immersing ourselves in life. It is a time to let go of pettiness and pretense.

No, working with grief and dying does not have to be depressing. Of course, it can be exhausting if the care of loved ones involves demanding around-the-clock duties, little sleep, extraordinary effort to relieve suffering, meticulous attention to the minute details of medication, and so on. And it can be difficult if, no matter what is done, the loved ones' condition continues to worsen or they and their families ride the roller coaster of positive reports and improvement, followed by negative reports and backsliding, followed by more improvement, followed by more worsening ... But it does not have to be depressing.

Working with grief and dying is difficult and exhausting when denial and aversion are present because the psychological and emotional effort required to push away Truth can completely sap the energy of everyone involved. The causes of our troubles doesn't come from the death or loss our loved one, but our steps to get rid of them are the causes. When we face it all openly and honestly, exploring the depths and subtleties of what loss, grief, and death have to teach us, the process can become profound. Sometimes it can even be humorous. At times, it even becomes joyous.

I do not mean to discount or trivialize the tremendous physical and emotional challenges that can be part and parcel of dying and loss. But it doesn't have to be an unrelieved tragedy.

Over many years I have learned that even the greatest tragedies in life can become the groundwork for tremendous growth and insight. Profound loss can be the catalyst for the shedding of old skin, the loosening of rigidity. Profound loss can pave the way for a new aliveness, a new enthusiasm, a totally new awareness.

I have seen dozens of people work with tragic and painful loss, with things so horrifying they seem completely unworkable. And slowly, eventually, many of those people come to a resolution of their feelings. In an astonishing number of cases, it's almost as if their lives have been strangely enhanced by an experience they wouldn't have wished on their worst enemies. Would they choose not to have had the experience? In most cases, yes, but the fact is they did have it, and they made a decision to work with what the Universe put on their plates, no matter how distasteful it may have been.

In conclusion, I would urge each and every person going through grief and loss to take things as they are now, instead of regretting what happened.

CHAPTER 07
FINDING PEACE

In this chapter we are going to talk about finding peace in any sort of grief, May it caused by death of a loved one, lack of success, or a wish never come true.

At some point in our lives, each of us has experienced moments of calm fulfillment, moments when everything seemed "okay," when our instinctive trust in the Universe came to the surface and we let down our guard and our defenses. We felt warmth, we felt peace, and we felt contentment. We breathed in deeply, our abdomens unusually relaxed, our shoulders uncharacteristically low. We breathed out a long, liberating exhale. The subtle fear was gone. The wariness had melted. The confusion and doubt had receded into irrelevance. We felt connected. We felt complete. We felt whole.

Some would say it felt like being in our mothers' arms, or back in the womb. Some would say it felt like a sense of "oneness" with nature or with the Universe. Some would say they forgot all their cares and just let go. Some would say it is the know-how and the understanding we were all born with in so many ways, we construct the conditions of our own suffering and then, when the suffering comes, we feel victimized by some outside force, or power, or individual.

Sometimes the grief in a relationship comes because a state of love, acceptance, and fulfillment was never achieved. Many of us have had extremely difficult relationships with our parents. If that is the case, our lives come to revolve, often subconsciously, around the process of attempting to resolve and complete whatever conflicts and incompleteness exist in those relationships.

It is possible and even common for an individual to spend an entire lifetime in a profound state of discontent, driven by an emptiness that dates back to some slight, some series of slights, or some offense that one or the other parent committed during the child's early years. A woman may spend her entire adult life habitually, mechanically sleeping with man after man after man all because her "inner child" longs for a love, affection, and acceptance she never got from her father.

And a man may spend decades amassing a fortune but never achieving happiness because he is driven to disprove a father who told him he would "never amount to anything." At a particular level, no matter how much money he has, he still fears that he "doesn't amount to anything." It is equally plausible that the same man might spend every day of his adult life sitting in barrooms and consuming quarts of whisky all because he believed his father.

Our grief may also arise out of the awareness, real or imagined that we have lost the possibility of having a good relationship because of age, illness, or being physically challenged. And if our sense of meaning in life has arisen from our ability to produce and achieve, the process of retirement may bring on a profound experience of grief as we wrestle with a loss of identity and direction.

Most people in the world are convinced that if they had more money, their worries would disappear. But people who have money suffer from an extraordinary fear of losing it; or worrying that it's not enough, that they need more and more and more to keep pace with inflation and to avoid suffering embarrassment as their friends, neighbors, and associates ascend higher and higher.

We look with awe upon those people in our society who we define as "driven." We admire them and compare ourselves to them, often wishing that we could cultivate the same level of "ambition" and dedicate ourselves to the same degree of accomplishment.

While it is possible to be single-mindedly devoted to a cause for humanitarian or philanthropic reasons or for the fulfillment of some personal dream or vision, more often people who are "driven" are motivated by some deep inner turmoil and sense of emptiness. Their manic drive to achieve and accomplish really grows out of a need to relieve their own inner discontent—their grief—in much the same manner as those of a different temperament might be inclined to drink their troubles away. Substance abuse and addiction, sexual addiction, power addiction, money addiction—all of these are expressions of unresolved grief, of a profound sense of loss and incompleteness.

I don't mean to suggest that there is no value in hard work. Nor do I mean to suggest that we shouldn't, at times, dedicate ourselves with a one-pointed focus toward the accomplishment of some heart-felt dream or the realization of some extremely meaningful personal goal. Hard work, discipline, and the ability to be focused are essential, invaluable tools for accomplishing one's life purpose, for leading a life that feels "full" and "meaningful" rather than "empty." The irony is that only through discipline can we achieve freedom.

One of the greatest grief's we can experience is the sense that we did less than we were capable of—in our relationships, in our world, and in our efforts to accomplish whatever our hearts encouraged us to accomplish. Simply stated, when we die or a loved one dies, as we reflect on our lives, or our relationships, we are usually much less concerned about what we did than about what we didn't do. On the other hand, as has been stated so often in recent years, when we are on our deathbeds we are usually not wishing we had spent more time at the office.

The key, most things is to find a balance, to get fulfillment in all tasks that we undertake instead of "sleepwalking" through life deserting things and those people who crucial to us, carelessly striving for an elusive sense of "success" and "achievement." Responsible, focused management of finances can eliminate much of the debilitating stress that surrounds financial hardship. It is not evil to make money, and it is wise to save it. But the "drive" we see in many people often arises out of less healthy, less conscious motives.

In general, everything our culture has told us and taught us about grief has exacerbated the problem instead of relieving it. In order to go successfully through this experience, we must unlearn much of what we learned about dealing with grief. Rather than pushing it away, rather than pretending it's not present, rather than keeping a stiff upper lip, we need to have the courage to cry, to sob, to open our hearts and allow ourselves to experience the pain, the wrath, the defeat, the anger, the intense sadness. We need to realize that we'll not drown in it all.

For a mother, it may have come through the experience of childbirth, of bringing another human being into the world. For others it may have come through romance, Or through a winning athletic effort or an outstanding artistic performance. Perhaps it came through scuba diving, skydiving, a scientific breakthrough, sex, mountain climbing, or just sitting by a stream or on the beach. It may have come at the moment we fell in love, or at the moment we lay in the grass staring up at the stars in the nighttime sky. It may have come in meditation or prayer, that evening in Paris, the gondola ride in Venice, the picnic in Central Park, being caressed and kissed by a school of fish while snorkeling, on the motorcycle ride down Pacific Coast Highway, in the moment he opened the mouth and uttered these words, "I love you."

At these moments, we surpass our limitations. And the state of expansiveness we move into is love. Since we have no fear, we have no anger because the two are intricately intertwined. When we're "in love," even people we don't like are suddenly okay. We may feel compassion for their predicament. There's no attraction to negativity because it separates and divides, and we are so content in our experience of merging.

But that very recognition, when the mind begins to focus on it, is terrifying. We've let down our defenses. We think, My Creator, I've allowed myself to be vulnerable. I am unprotected. I am out of my mind! Come back to earth. Get hold of yourself. Come to your senses. And suddenly we are again separate and frightened.

We return to the comfortable familiarity of our fears. We sacrifice bliss and joy and aliveness to feel "safe." For a moment our minds quieted and our hearts opened and we expanded into larger, less defined beings, with a spirit of playfulness and freedom. But as soon as our minds "kicked in," they told us we were in insecure territory.

Later, we remember the experience and we desperately want to recapture it. But the problem is that we are using our minds to create the experience again ... and our minds want to come along this time. We want the bliss, but we also want the "safety" of our judging minds.

So we become addicted to whatever the method was that got us into that state of expanded awareness in the first place. We want to do it all the time. And if it was other people who got us there, we want to be with them all the time, and to protect them and ensure that they won't fall into danger ... or the arms of another.

Our grief is the agony that is generated by this effort to control. It's the conceptualizing of a "perfect" Universe—one in which everything and everyone is just as we want—and then the resistance to the way things and people really are.

If we think back on our moments of bliss and contentment, we would very likely remember that they came unexpectedly, not as a result of something we had designed for ourselves, but as a result of a surprising development, an unforeseen turn of events and emotions. We may have practiced our golf swing for years, but the day we first broke eighty on the golf course our feelings of intense satisfaction were experienced not so much as the end result of all our training, but rather as a magical unlocking of the doorway to fulfillment inside us that had previously been sealed shut.

Similarly, when we "fall in love" the feeling often washes over us at an unexpected moment. It is a "high" unlike any we've ever felt. And though the physical and mental images of our beloved are connected to the unfolding of the experience, and that experience is still inside of us.

The foundations of our grief are built in our minds' misperception that the experience of love was fed into us from outside—that we can only have it if the people who triggered it are present in our lives in the way we want them to be, or the circumstances of our lives are exactly as we have designed them in our minds.

We don't acknowledge how vulnerable we are ... we want things the way we want them. We don't recognize the improbability of our lives—and the people in them—working out the way we want them to. It's almost as if we constantly climb up a tree on the edge of a cliff, make our way out to a thin, fragile branch that overhangs the canyon, jump up and down on that skinny, fragile branch, and then shout out, "I am going to be certainly upset if this branch breaks and I fall into the chasm."

In so many ways, we construct the conditions of our own suffering and then, when the suffering comes, we feel victimized by some outside force, or power, or individual.

Sometimes the grief in a relationship comes because a state of love, acceptance, and fulfillment was never achieved. Many of us have had extremely difficult relationships with our parents. If that is the case, our lives come to revolve, often subconsciously, around the process of attempting to resolve and complete whatever conflicts and incompleteness exist in those relationships.

It is possible and even common for an individual to spend an entire lifetime in a profound state of discontent, driven by an emptiness that dates back to some slight, some series of slights, or some offense that one or the other parent committed during the child's early years. A woman may spend her entire adult life habitually, mechanically sleeping with man after man after man all because her "inner child" longs for a love, affection, and acceptance she never got from her father.

And a man may spend decades amassing a fortune but never achieving happiness because he is driven to disprove a father who told him he would "never amount to anything." At a particular level, no matter how much money he has, he still fears that he "doesn't amount to anything." It is equally plausible that the same man might spend every day of his adult life sitting in barrooms and consuming quarts of whisky all because he believed his father.

Our grief may also arise out of the awareness, real or imagined that we have lost the possibility of having a good relationship because of age, illness, or being physically challenged. And if our sense of meaning in life has arisen from our ability to produce and achieve, the process of retirement may bring on a profound experience of grief as we wrestle with a loss of identity and direction.

Most people in the world are convinced that if they had more money, their worries would disappear. But people who have money suffer from an extraordinary fear of losing it; or worrying that it's not enough, that they need more and more and more to keep pace with inflation and to avoid suffering embarrassment as their friends, neighbors, and associates ascend higher and higher.

We look with awe upon those people in our society who we define as "driven." We admire them and compare ourselves to them, often wishing that we could cultivate the same level of "ambition" and dedicate ourselves to the same degree of accomplishment.

While it is possible to be single-mindedly devoted to a cause for humanitarian or philanthropic reasons or for the fulfillment of some personal dream or vision, more often people who are "driven" are motivated by some deep inner turmoil and sense of emptiness. Their manic drive to achieve and accomplish really grows out of a need to relieve their own inner discontent—their grief—in much the same manner as those of a different temperament might be inclined to drink their troubles away. Substance abuse and addiction, sexual addiction, power addiction, money addiction—all of these are expressions of unresolved grief, of a profound sense of loss and incompleteness.

I don't mean to suggest that there is no value in hard work. Nor do I mean to suggest that we shouldn't, at times, dedicate ourselves with a one-pointed focus toward the accomplishment of some heart-felt dream or the realization of some extremely meaningful personal goal. Hard work, discipline, and the ability to be focused are essential, invaluable tools for accomplishing one's life purpose, for leading a life that feels full and meaningful relatively than empty. The irony is that only through discipline can we achieve freedom.

One of the greatest grief's we can experience is the sense that we did less than we were capable of—in our relationships, in our world, and in our efforts to accomplish whatever our hearts encouraged us to accomplish. Simply stated, when we die or a loved one dies, as we reflect on our lives, or our relationships, we are usually much less concerned about what we did than about what we didn't do. On the other hand, as has been stated so often in recent years, when we are on our deathbeds we are usually not wishing we had spent more time at the office.

Our hearts are our lifelines. If we respond in fear and close them, we miss the healing potential and solace they offer. Our hearts have no boundaries—they are immeasurable. The only limits they have are the ones our minds impose on them.

The healing of grief begins when we permit our hearts to be open and susceptible, when we allow ourselves into them, and allow our wounds and sorrows to be cured by them. While our traditional conditioning has been to close our hearts at times of sadness or fear, the true curing takes place when we open them to absorb our belatedness, and swallow it into the infinite light they contain.

The miracle is that our very individual hearts bid us the chance for development, for completeness, for forgiveness, for nurturing, and for the realization of infinite opportunities. Real fulfillment is found inside ourselves. It isn't dependent on the presence of, or actions of, anyone else. It isn't dependent on the acquisition of material possessions and wealth. Each loss, each place of emptiness, each unresolved grief, each resentment, and each failure can be healed in the infinite mercy of our own hearts.

CHAPTER 08
DETOURS ARE FRUSTRATING

The second task of grief is that you experience all the emotions associated with the death of your loved one. Grief consists of a number of emotions that need to be honestly and freely expressed. If they are not acknowledged and become internalized, that can lead to emotional or physical problems later on.

In grieving you need to be aware of both your thoughts and your feelings. One widower came to us after reading one of our books, Getting to the Other Side of Grief, which deals with grief following the death of a spouse. He claimed that he had read the entire book and done all the exercises but still didn't feel any better. After asking a few questions, we learned that his wife had died only three months earlier and that he had approached his grieving like he did his job as an efficiency consultant to organizations! He had taken the to- tally cognitive, rational approach. He read the book, followed the suggestions, and thought he should be better. He didn't understand that he needed to deal with his feelings and that this process couldn't be rushed. Working through all of your feelings takes time, which is the other critical factor you need along with doing grief work in order to journey through grief.

There are three things to remember about the connection between your emotions and your grief. First, you need to realize that emotions are natural responses to all kinds of situations. We all have feelings. We don't have to justify them to others. They just exist. Remember how we said earlier that our emotions and thoughts often conflict with each other while we are grieving? This task of grief challenges you to be very intentional about differentiating between your thoughts and feelings. Thoughts can be debated, and you can argue with someone else to defend your thinking. While grieving, most of us don't really like to get into that. We just want what we say to be respected. That's why it is often preferable to tell people how you feel rather than what you think. So remember to identify and talk about your feelings.

Not only are emotions a natural response to your loss, but they are also healthy. We all have emotions that we may label as negative like sad and mad. But they are not wrong. They are neither good nor bad. They just are. Normally people associate the emotion of sadness with being a bad thing or something to quickly change. After all, we live in a culture that continually tells us we should be happy and not worry.

So when people hear that sadness and anger are really nor- mal feelings and that they don't need to flee from them but rather embrace and experience them, they are sometimes understandably reluctant to actually do that. However, you will undoubtedly have negative feelings while grieving, and learning how to deal with those feelings in a healthy way is a necessary thing to do.

Second, we believe that people need to decide how to respond to their emotions. We often use the image of a bottle to represent the receptacle where emotions go if they are internalized. If a person swallows feelings by not allowing for their expression, those feelings do not go away. Instead they are being stored. They accumulate in the bottle, and when the bottle gets too full, feelings can manifest themselves in a variety of undesirable ways, such as depression, anxiety, or a physical illness.

It is healthiest to be congruent in expressing your thoughts and, even more so, your feelings to those involved with your grief issues. The principle of congruence calls for honesty and integrity in assertively stating what you think and feel, and then behaving by your words and actions in ways consistent with your thoughts and feelings. So, be congruent by not pretending you are okay when you're not, especially when others ask how you're doing. It is healthiest to express emotions honestly rather than to tell people what you think they'd like to hear. Remember that if emotions are honestly and openly expressed and dealt with, you can eventually work through them, and they will dissipate as you let them go. Doing that may also make you more vulnerable to others, but in the process it draws you closer, and you can hopefully feel even more connected with them.

Third, feelings are so individual that you should not expect others to have or express them in the same way. So don't be afraid to be truly you in what and how you communicate.

Your gender influences your emotional expression as well. Both men and women may experience some similar emotions of grief, but stereotypically they express their feelings differently. Men tend to be more closed, often trying to appear strong and in control because they have been taught that "real men" do not cry. Women, on the other hand, tend to be more openly expressive. Crying is more often expected and accepted in females, according to traditional societal norms. We would encourage you to recognize that combining traditionally masculine and feminine characteristics provides the healthiest approach to grieving for both men and women. So give appropriate expression to your emotions based on your own unique personality, gender, and

DETOURS ARE FRUSTRATING

culture so the emotions won't accumulate and eventually cause damage. One of the most prevalent reasons why a person might get stuck on the grief detour is that their emotional receptacle is overflowing with swallowed or sup- pressed feelings. Don't let that happen to you. Honestly express your feelings so they can get out!

CHAPTER 09
SAYING GOOD-BYE TO THE OLD ROAD

Realistically Summarizing Your Life with the Deceased and Storing the Memories

Memories are reminders of the past that live on in our minds and hearts. They represent that portion of life that is now past. You undoubtedly have already stored many memories of your deceased loved one from your life together. They now reside in your memory and can be recalled at will. You move on, and you remember.

The third task on the grief journey is to find a place for memories of the person who died that honors what you had together and acknowledges who you are now because of your relationship, but also makes room for you to move on. This task will help you further understand and implement task one by accepting the "historical" aspect of your relationship with the deceased, and it adds an entirely new dimension to the grief journey. That is to say, whatever relationship you may have had with that person has now ended. It is in the past. It will never come back, but it has given you the gift of memories.

How do we create memories? Memories begin with the actual events or experiences we have by ourselves or with others. When the actual event is over, we have collected all kinds of information, feelings, and associations that are now stored in our minds—in our memories. These memories can be "awakened" either by our intentional recall of the event or by some other trigger like hearing a song or seeing a picture that brings the memory into our awareness. Memories are important to us because they are evidence of what our lives consisted of. They are the story of the life we lived with our loved ones.

Memories don't just "happen" to us. While we subconsciously store memories, we can also be very intentional about creating memories. We "memorize" things. So one of the biggest emotional challenges you face on your grief detour is taking the relationship you had with your loved one and now translating it all into memories.

Reviewing everything, including possessions of the deceased and places you went with the person, will assist you in this process. Doing this refreshes your memories for easy retrieval. What is especially challenging for many people is the mistaken notion that if they accept the reality of the death and begin to put this person in the past, somehow the memories of that person will fade. They think they will forget their loved one. Of course, that is not the case any more than we would forget any of the other important people and events in our lives. But here is another example of how emotions can often rule over the mind. We can become so afraid that we will forget that we actually believe it will happen, even though our minds tell us that this will not be the case.

Not all memories are pleasant, so what do you do with the unpleasant ones you might have of your loved one? You may actually want to forget some aspects of your relationship with the person who died, or you might think you will be disloyal to a person who is not here to shield himself or herself if you say or think something negative about that person. We all realize that no one is perfect. Our personalities are a composite of everything we are—the good and the not-so-good.

So remember this person realistically—the good and the bad together. If you don't do that, you will put that person on a pedestal and make moving through your grief that much harder or even impossible.

The difficulty of moving the deceased to the past and storing memories of him or her is that you need to say good-bye and let go of that person. Your loved one is no longer a part of your present life, and you won't be able to move on if you're still holding on to someone who now really belongs in your past. Saying good-bye and letting go doesn't mean that the relationship was not important to you. It has nothing to do with how much you loved the person. People who had healthy and happy relationships often have less difficulty letting go after honorably and heartily grieving than those with conflicted relationships, so commence to find means to say goodbye once more and again until you can truly move that person to your past, and he or she becomes a series of treasured memories that you can easily recall.

There is one other primary way your loved one can stay close to you in addition to your collection of memories of him or her. You are likely a different person in some specific ways because of how this person impacted your life. He or she may have deeply influenced your beliefs, your values, your religious faith, your habits and customs, and your lifestyle. Perhaps you enjoy certain activities partially because this person had introduced you to them. You may find yourself reflecting on how your loved one influenced and changed your life. You may hear yourself saying, "I wouldn't be doing this or be involved in that if it weren't for name!"

So in addition to your reminiscences, you currently have a life perspective and a lifestyle that has been deeply affected because he or she was a part of your life. Who you are now includes those influences of all the people who have been close to you, for they have in some sense become a part of you, and you take all of that with you throughout your life.

Specific Ways to Work on Your Grief

Over time, if you are the person closest to the deceased, go through all your loved one's possessions, remembering how the person looked and behaved and the times you had together. Recall their love for various activities or interests.

When you look through your loved one's clothing and all the other things he or she acquired, you will be cementing your memories of that person. You will begin to put that person in your past, realizing that your loved one will never use the clothes or all the other possessions again. There may be some items you wish to keep in a memory box to look at from time to time or on special occasions to remember the deceased person. Some of these may be items you want to keep until the time seems right to give them to another family member as a special keepsake. You now face the need to accept the reality that your loved one isn't coming back, and in doing so you will continue the process of letting go.

> Review and edit all the pictures, videos, slides, and other memorabilia. Make a picture book, scrapbook, or memory book of the life you and your deceased loved one had together. Put it where you can look at it frequently to recall your memories.

> Summarize your loved one's life realistically; don't "sanitize" their memory. Think and speak about your loved one accurately in both positive and negative ways. Eventually be able to identify not only all the positives but some of the

things that you do not miss about the deceased, such as now you don't have to go to a restaurant you didn't care for, or watch science fiction movies when you prefer comedies.

Put your relationship with the deceased on a lifeline. Actually draw a line (maybe you'll need to tape pages together) and plot your birth date and other significant points in your life on that line. Include the beginning of your relationship with the deceased as well as their death to see where it began and where it now ends. Mark and label all the other significant times you had with your loved one. Your life needs to move on, so make sure your line extends beyond the point of your loved one's death. You have more things to experience and accomplish in this world even if right now you have no idea what those things might be.

Write a story of your relationship with the deceased from its beginning to the time of their death. Include in that story such things as your predominant memories, what you valued most and least about the relationship, and how your life has been affected because of your relationship together.

Identify and incorporate ways your deceased loved one enhanced your life, and how you are different because you were their spouse, child, parent, sibling, or friend. In other words, as you move through your grief journey you will be able to determine how you grew because of your relationship with that person.

Visit places that were special in your relationship together, such as restaurants, vacation spots, parks, or beaches.

Remember the times you spent together there. Do many of the same things that were special to the two of you or your family without the person who died. This is often a very difficult and emotional experience, but so very important.

It helps you recall events, disempowers the place somewhat each time you revisit it, and helps you decide if you still like it without your deceased loved one. When you go to these special places or are with people who were significant to you and your loved one, be aware of the empty place previously occupied by your loved one. That will help you remember, relive events, and then decide if you still want to do that activity or be with those people without your deceased loved one.

Celebrate the positive aspects of your loved one's life by listening to the tape of the tributes friends and family had given at the funeral. Reread comments or stories that people had written about your loved one, and read things you may have written yourself about him or her. You might ask family and friends to write down their favorite stories or ways they appreciated this person so you can put them in a memory book to help honor and remember the person who died.

Use the past tense as much as possible to refer to the de-ceased. That means "was" rather than "is," because the relationship no longer has a present or a future. If your child died, talk about things that belonged (past tense) to your child while she or he was alive. Your loved one is no longer living and physically present.

Use any religious, cultural, or family ritual that emphasizes the transition of the relationship from a present reality to an honored memory. This may be a candle-lighting ceremony, a toast, the singing of a favorite song, reading a special story or Scripture passage, making the person's favorite food, or participating in a memorial event, but especially emphasize the "we remember" and "in the past" features of the ritual.

Be familiar with many ways and times you will need to say good-bye to your loved one before you have completed the detour of grieving. Write in a letter to your deceased loved one on special occasions how you feel about the prospect of spending the day without him or her. You can write things like, "You will never be here again to celebrate Christmas with me. I hate that thought, but I need to say good-bye to our Christmas times together."

Offer a gift to a donations or special cause in memory of your loved one. This becomes a tangible way to memorialize the person and benefit a special interest he or she had.

Be cautious about using websites that invite people to post messages to deceased loved ones as if active communication were still possible. Real communication involves two physically present people who can exchange thoughts and feelings together. We discourage any type of Internet connection that suggests the possibility that your deceased loved one can actually receive or respond to correspondence you may send. However, we certainly encourage writing journal letters to the deceased as a therapeutic expression.

Know that you will never forget your loved one, but you will eventually remember that person free from the pain of your grief. When you are no longer in pain that will be one of several signals that you probably have come to the end of your grief detour and have finished your grieving

CHAPTER 10
SETTING MY SIGHTS ON A NEW DIRECTION

Getting to Know Who You Are Now
Simply stated, the fourth task of grief is to adjust to life by deciding who you are as an individual without your deceased loved one. As a bereaved person, you need to recognize that your life is ultimately an individual journey. Your life may have been so closely linked to your deceased loved one that it is difficult to realize that you are your own unique person. It may feel like a part of you is missing. Now you must (re)define yourself after your loved one's death. This is predominantly challenging for almost all bereaved people. For a bereaved spouse it means accommodating that you are now single without a partner, and yet you are still a whole, complete individual. Or, if you were a parent, you may no longer function as such following your child's death if you have no other children. Likewise, you will no longer be a child to anyone when both of your parents have died, or a sibling if you have no other living brothers or sisters. If you had one best friend, you no lon-

ger have that best friend. Death changes the roles we play, and those roles help define us.

Now you also need to reevaluate the various interests and activities you participated in because of, or with, the person who died. Will you continue to do those things (such as boating, attending the theater, helping out at school, or going to sports events) now that your loved one is no longer here to participate with you? You must to examine yourself, "Who was I before my extinct loved one came into the picture?" "Who was I with that loved one?" "Who am I now without that person in my life?" And eventually the question will be- come, "Who am I now?"

Figuring out who you are independent of your deceased loved one is a necessary part of getting through this grief detour. Other people might come alongside you to offer comfort and support, but you need to take charge of your life and figure out who you are now. The principle behind this task, regardless of what type of loss you have experienced, is quite simple but also very profound: we are all individual persons, whole and complete in and of ourselves. We don't need another person to make us whole or complete, even though we may want people around to enhance our lives. Certainly we grow together in our marriages, or we live in special relationships with our children, siblings, or parents. We all are social beings to some extent, although some like to be surrounded by people more than others. But we must recognize that by birth we are complete persons by ourselves and capable as adults of living without any one specific person in our lives.

This fourth task means you recognize that you have a life independent of the one you had with the deceased person. That person obviously impacted the contours of your life. But you now need to begin finding ways to reinvest in life on your own terms without that person. You will have to begin making decisions without considering the one who died.

This fourth task, then, addresses the need for you to evaluate where you feel painfully empty because of your past connection with the deceased, determine how you want to fill that emptiness, and reconstruct your own identity without a relationship with that person. You have to work at knowing and loving yourself, discovering and engaging in your own interests and activities, developing a renewed caring for others, and determining your own life purposes now.

Specific Ways to Work on Your Grief

1) Write down and analyze what roles you will and will no longer play following the death of your loved one. Draw a circle and section off all the roles you play in your life, including those you had with your deceased loved one. Cut the circle like a pie into pieces the size of the role investment you made, for example, as a spouse, parent, adult child, sibling, co-worker, friend, and with yourself. This will help you see how much time and energy you devoted to each relationship and how big a space the deceased person occupied in your life—this is the primary area that now needs reconstruction and development.

2) After you recognize what roles your deceased loved one played in your life, you will have to determine how you will compensate for that loss. Listing the roles or writing them in a letter to your deceased loved one may be very helpful, saying, for example, "These are all the ways you contributed to my life to my benefit. Thank you so much, but now I have to determine how to manage these things without you." Then initiate to explore methods to fill the voids.

3) Identify your own personal interests and activities and how they compare with those of the person who died. You will no longer need to consider their interests in making your plans.

4) Now you can personally decide if you want to pursue any of those things your deceased loved one enjoyed. Feeling

compelled to continue something only out of a sense of loyalty is not healthy or helpful.

5) Recognize that you are an important person whose thoughts, feelings, and ideas really do matter. Revisit the hopes and dreams you had before this person was in your life. Look at who you are becoming as you learn more about yourself on this grief detour. Grieving is a growth process in which you become more aware of what is important and gain a clearer sense of direction and purpose. This means that changes are occurring. Don't allow people to pressure you back into an old mold. Take a break from some of your prior activities to explore other options you have. Try new things before deciding what you like and want in your life now.

6) Analyze other social and family relationships and decide which ones you want to maintain or enhance. Each individual relationship requires time for it. Following the death of your loved one, you now have the time that relationship took available for other things. However, you also have to compensate for all the things your loved one did, especially if he or she lived with you. Eventually you will probably want to invest in other and new relationships, but do not do this at the expense of your journey through the grief detour. We are talking mostly about friendships, but if you have been widowed and are considering dating, our strong recommendation is that you wait at least a year before beginning to date and also that you be certain you are finished grieving first. A person needs to feel single and whole again and accept the fact that the relationship with the deceased is over before moving into another romantic relationship. Remember that it takes time and energy to work on the tasks of grieving. Make that your first priority before pursuing other arenas.

7) Recognize that insecurity and a lack of confidence are normal when you try to determine who you are right now. Part of your self-confidence may have been fueled by the support you

received from the person who died. Without that validation, a sense of personal inadequacy and a lower level of self-esteem can creep in. Make encouraging comments to yourself about your own qualities, abilities, and worth. You are a good person. You do have many capabilities. Figure out who you are and be your own person.

8) Know that you can wait a while to select a gravestone. Your funeral director can put a temporary marker at the grave site, so you can decide later about something permanent. Many surviving spouses tend to choose a double headstone at the time of death because of the closeness they experienced with their spouse. However, you may realize (especially if you are relatively young) that a decision made too early may be solely an emotional one. Choosing a dual headstone may sometimes conflict with a healthy separation from the deceased or detract from realizing that your life will eventually go on.

Many people erroneously believe they will be reunited in the afterlife, and they want to try to maintain an unbroken connection with a deceased spouse through a shared headstone. We believe it is healthiest to realize your marriage is now over before making any decision regarding a headstone. Selecting a single headstone in no way eliminates the choice to someday be buried next to your deceased spouse.

9) Realize that "getting back to normal" as soon as possible is not a healthy goal. Grieving takes time and work, and busyness is an avoidance or distraction to the process. You need to decide what suits you now. Give yourself the grief assignments that you have been reading about. Set specific time aside to do them.

Rushing through the process isn't helpful. Know that the "old" normal will never return—you must develop a "new" normal life pattern. The old pattern involved your deceased loved one who is no longer here. Now you need to develop your new life pattern—changed at least by the fact that you have one less person whom you love in your life.

10) Realize that your life will go on. Even though you may feel awful right now, as though your life died with your loved one, trust that your life will improve with both the passing of time and your intentional grief work.

CHAPTER 11
HEADING FOR A CLEAR ROAD AHEAD

Plotting a New Route for Your Journey Just like wanting a detour to end, you are probably eager to be done grieving. Wouldn't it be nice to just snap your fingers and feel better, free from the pain of your loss and filled with enthusiasm for the future? Grieving, as you undoubtedly realize by now, doesn't work that way. But, just as with a de- tour, you aren't rerouted forever. Eventually you do get back to the main road. The route won't be exactly like it was be- fore you were detoured by your grief. But the time will come when you are feeling better and are somewhat eagerly mapping out where you want to go when your detour finally comes to an end.

The fifth and final task of grief is to reinvest fully in life. As you separate your identity from that of your deceased loved one, you are setting the course for your journey as an individual without the person who died. Your life may look very different than it did before. The death of your loved one has changed a multitude of things. The old ways no longer fit because you must now do things without him or her. Obviously, the degree of change depends on the level of connection you had with the person who died. You may decide to continue heading in somewhat the same direction as before, but nevertheless your life will still look and feel different in some ways.

This final task is one of reinvesting in your "new normal" life as you reluctantly bid farewell to the old standard. It may appear to you similar standing on the deck of a cruise ship, waving good-bye to a loved one you will miss, but also being eager to discover what lies ahead of you on your trip. Because these tasks are not linear or sequential, reinvestment in life as an individual without your deceased loved one will happen in a number of little ways as you grieve. Relief and reassurance often come in small doses—each time you say or think, "I still like this" or "I can really do this on my own."

A primary goal of this task is to realize and accept that you have more life to live and to reinvest in it so that you do not become a "professional" griever. Research suggests that around 85 percent of bereaved people are able to establish a renewed life pattern without getting stuck in their grief. "Getting stuck" means not accepting the reality of your loss or emotionally letting go of your grief. You certainly will remember your grief (and, of course, the deceased person). You will even remember having the pain—but the pain itself will no longer be present. Moments may still come when sadness and perhaps a few tears briefly return, especially during major events or transitions such as marriages, graduations, other deaths, births of children or grandchildren, and the like. However, the pain likely will not be as intense or last as long as when you were grieving. You can get to the point where you can say that as far as you can determine you are done grieving, at least for now. We would then also encourage you to share that belief with others to help them under- stand you now are ready to move on.

You will have achieved a major goal when you have worked through your grief. Certainly, grieving has been difficult and painful. But your grief also ends. If you have worked on your grief, you have every reason to believe that within one to three years after your loved one's death (if there are no complicating factors), you will have healed and moved into a renewed vital life. While you will not be the same as you were before, many of the major features of your life will probably be similar. We often use the analogy of remodeling a house. Some renovations are relatively small and simple; others are more extensive. But in any case, you do not actually tear down the entire house and build a new one.

The grief journey involves some level of renovation. In many ways you are still the same person, but your life is not as it was previously because the place your loved one once occupied is now empty. You can't go back to yesterday. You are in the process of finding a new normal to your life—life without your loved one. And grief will change you in new and different ways. But you won't be worse for the wear, although it may feel like that for a while. You can now begin to see new possibilities not only for the present but also for your future.

Reinvesting fully in life is a continual process that focuses on the questions "Who am I currently?" from the fourth task) and "How do I want to live my life now that my loved one has died?" from this fifth job. These two tasks imply a challenge as these questions begin to flow shortly after your loved one died and continue throughout your grief process.

That is one reason why returning too quickly to your previous activities, involvements, commitments, social groups, and even full-time work (if financially you can initially take time off from work) is not really the most desirable thing to do.

We know that our society does not like to see people in pain. Other people may breathe a sigh of relief when they see you returning to some of what was once "normal" rather than being focused on grieving and working on the tasks of grief. But remember, you are in charge of your life, so do yourself a huge favor and give yourself the time to grieve.

Grieving at the time your loved one dies is definitely healthier than waiting until some later time. You will still have to actively deal with your grief no matter how long you wait.

Grief doesn't go away on its own. Be intentional about working on the tasks of grief. Only by attending to them will you be able to put your deceased loved one in your past and truly reinvest in life in a new, full, and complete way. You Know You Are Done Grieving When You . . .

- can talk about your deceased loved one and recall special memories without crying or feeling significant pain.
- have removed all of his or her clothes and other personal belongings from closets and drawers and have claimed those spaces for your own use if that person had lived with you, have made decisions about disposing of or using these things, and perhaps have placed some keep-sakes in a memory box to store.
- have no rooms or places that could constitute a shrine to your deceased loved one.
- have rearranged furniture and pictures the way you want them and now have only a few pictures on display of your deceased loved one.
- can look at pictures of your loved one and remember both the positives and negatives of that person and your relationship with him or her.
- can go out with the friends, couples, and families you went with before (if you still desire to do so) and feel good about yourself without your deceased loved one.
- have developed new relationships with other people, such as with some single individuals if you were widowed, or perhaps others who have experienced similar losses (such as the death of a child, parent, sibling, or friend).

Grief and Loss

- have revisited all your significant and memorable places without your loved one to remember and store those memories and to evaluate whether that is still a place you want to claim as your own.
- enjoy doing things your deceased loved one would not have participated in.
- no longer do things you didn't enjoy but had done with and for the deceased because he or she wanted to.
- have developed and are comfortable with your own decision-making process.
- are energized by your new or renewed sense of direction.
- can be by yourself and not feel lonely or yearn for your deceased loved one.
- have dealt with all the feelings (such as anger, guilt, remorse, regret, and sadness) that you may have felt about your relationship with the deceased.
- feel like you are a whole and complete person in yourself.
- can look in the mirror and smile at yourself and believe you will be all right.
- feel you have something to contribute to others.
- can recognize the positive aspects of being where you are in your life after grieving.
- know you are important and can be kind and caring to yourself by cooking nice meals, traveling, doing fun things, taking walks, and the like.
- believe you have completed the tasks of grief and have said good-bye for the last time.
- are satisfied and content with your life as it is now going.

In addition, if you were widowed, you also know you are done grieving when you:

- have removed your wedding ring from the fourth finger of your left hand and have decided what you will do with the ring.
- have devised a way to manage your sexuality appropriate to your value system.

- are comfortable checking the box single on forms and can squeeze some of the gains of being single.

Specific Ways to Work on Your Grief

1) Work through your grief. Assess where you are at this point.

Grief is not a dead-end street or a cul-de-sac. You can get to the other side and no longer feel the acute pain. You may have occasional moments of sadness, but the devastating pain of intense grief will eventually be gone. You can once again feel good about yourself and excited about your life.

2) Make certain the pain is gone, and if not, identify what still triggers the pain. Review the activities and behaviors of the various tasks of grief that address your pain. Keep working on those areas until they no longer hurt. Hurting is a sign that you have not yet healed completely. Especially reread the section on desensitization in chapter 2 if you still experience pain in doing certain things. When doing something that is still painful, listen to what you are saying to yourself about that situation. Make certain you use positive self-talk, like, "In the activity, so I will find new ways to enjoy it at the moment."

3) As you go through the anguish process, identify what will now be part of your "new normal" life pattern. What interests, activities, volunteer time, or work do you want to pursue?

How is that the same or different than before your loved one died?

4) Journal about what your loved one's death and your grieving process have taught you. Develop ways to live more fully through what you have learned and have become. Grieving will change you. You do grow through grief, that is, if you use it to help yourself grow. Perhaps you will appreciate the little things more or not get bent out of shape as easily when something goes wrong.

Hope you realize that although grief is a long and difficult detour on your life journey, you do not have to experience this grief for the rest of your life. Get a healthy start on grieving beginning with the funeral events and work on your grief consistently until you reach a satisfying finish. In assessing your progress, determine what you still need to do by referring to the lists of specific ways to work on your grief at the end of the mental health sections in the previous chapters, and use the preceding section on "You Know You

Are Done Grieving at your a final checklist. If you have followed these recommendations, no longer feel the pain of your loved one's death, and have gone through at least the first anniversary of the death (all four seasons), you may be ready to declare yourself to be finished grieving (as far as you can tell).

However, don't be discouraged if you think you still have a long way to go before being totally finished. Remember, grieving typically takes one to three years, and sometimes a little longer, before you are through the detour. Once you say, "Yes, I think I am through weeping!" then the in good physical shape thing is to deliberately tell others your good news. Go "public" with your significant accomplishment. But do remember that coming to the end of your grief detour requires both an emotional readiness and a willful resolve to be done grieving and to move into your new life.

CHAPTER 12
MOVING ON

Once you have gone through the various stages of grief, moving on should become easier.
Grief has a lot of facets.
Here are some tips on how to move on:

- No one can go through that grief aside from you. No one, not even your closest friend or you parents can tell you how to handle grief. No one can tell what to feel. It is your sole responsibility.
- Grief has its own purpose. You need to go through the process so you can learn to accept everything that has happened. Losing someone or something important to you can be devastating but it is an experience where you can learn a lot from.
- Believe that this phase will be over soon. This is not a permanent feeling. Sooner or later you will heal and you will recover. No one gets stuck in sadness and emptiness forever.
- You have to take care of yourself. Grief can take its toll on your health and you might succumb to stress and anxiety.

MOVING ON

Dealing with a roller coaster of emotions while attending to arrangements can be stressful. Make sure that you take a break once in a while to recharge your energy.

- Take care of your health. Some people turn to food for comfort, it is referred to as emotional eating. This will not be good to your health and might result to obesity and other more serious medical conditions.
- Sharing your thoughts is good therapy. Whatever it is you are feeling, it is best if you talk to someone about it. When you talk with someone, it can somehow help ease your pain. People say that shared pain is easier to manage than the pain that you keep to yourself. Your friends and family will understand, so you just have to be honest about your true feelings.
- While it helps to be around your friends and family, it would also help if you find some time to be on your own. Why not take your family out for the weekend to somewhere you haven't been before, or you can travel alone. A vacation is a good way to ease stress.
- A loss can derail your route. It takes you away from your normal routine. Counselors say that it is best if you continue on with your normal activities. Do not alter what you usually do just because you are grieving, as much as possible, stick to your routines.
- It is perfectly all right to ask for help. Admitting that you are in pain is your first step to full recovery. Do not hesitate to ask for help because you cannot overcome this stage alone. It is okay to spend some time alone once in a while, but do not isolate yourself. The people around you will understand that you cannot be self-sufficient at this stage. Let the people who want to help you do their part.
- While it is good to learn new things and explore other options, now is not the best time make major decisions and extreme life changes. Wait until you have restored a sense of balance into your life before making life altering decisions and/

Grief and Loss

or ventures. Do not make decisions in spur-of the-moment situations; you might regret them in the long run.

- Grief is a process. You don't overcome pain and improve in just weeks or months. Some individuals even take them years to fully recover. Do not rush into it; you need to process your feelings to better handle them.
- Keep in mind that grief may be painful but it cannot harm. It is a very difficult situation but you will soon survive and when you look back, you will just smile at how you were able to handle grief.
- Do not regret anything
- Do not be surprised if you regress a little during the process. It is a normal thing when you are going through the process. Trust that it will not last long.
- It is okay to be reminded of the anniversary. Deaths are painful and whenever anniversaries happen, all the more that you will feel the pain of your loss.

CONCLUSION

Once the initial reaction of shock and denial, there come a whole lot of other emotions; One is anger and a feeling of hopelessness for not having control over things, Anger at people who caused the loss. Then, depression and sadness set in. When you are able to understand your emotions and why you are feeling that way you are feeling, you will be on your way to resolution and recovery.

- Putting into words, your fears, thoughts, and feelings is a good therapy. It is another way of acknowledging the pain as you go through it.
- Do not isolate yourself. You need support and the people around you are willing to give you that. Reconnect with friends and family. Join support groups in your church or community.
- Participate in a new sport or hobby. Volunteer in one of your church's outreach activities.
- Go on vacation. Have some alone time.
- Accept your grief. It is okay to admit that you are in pain and that you need help.
- Create new opportunities. Remember that if God closes a door, He will surely open a window.

CONCLUSION

- Get in touch with your spiritual side. Take a sabbatical. Attend retreats for spiritual renewal.
- Do not worry. Let the normal grieving process take its course. No need to rush, you will get there eventually.

Printed in Great Britain
by Amazon